THE TREASURES OF

William Shakespeare

CATHERINE M S ALEXANDER

ANDRE
DEUTSCH

CONTENTS

AUTHOR'S ACKNOWLEDGEMENTS
I should like to thank my colleagues at the Shakespeare Institute of the University of Birmingham and those who curate the collections of the Shakespeare Birthplace Trust and the Royal Shakespeare Company, but most of all, my thanks go to EA and WMA for their support for my labours.

All quotations are from the Oxford Shakespeare edited by Stanley Wells and Gary Taylor (1988).

THIS IS AN ANDRE DEUTSCH BOOK

Royal Shakespeare Company logo ™ The Royal Shakespeare Company, Stratford-Upon-Avon
Design copyright © André Deutsch Limited 2006, 2014
Text copyright © Catherine M. S. Alexander 2006, 2014

First published in 2006 as *Shakespeare: The Life, The Works, The Treasures*

This edition published in 2014 by André Deutsch,
An imprint of the Carlton Publishing Group
20 Mortimer Street
London, W1T 3JW

Printed in China
All rights reserved
A CIP catalogue for this book is available from the British Library

ISBN: 978-0-233-00417-4

INTRODUCTION

William Shakespeare is the best-known dramatist in the world and his plays, plots, characters and language have outlived their original context of the Elizabethan and Jacobean playhouses.

The playwright Ben Jonson, writing a memorial verse for his friend in the First Folio of 1623, declared that Shakespeare was "The applause, delight, the wonder of our stage", but added, "He was not of an age, but for all time". He cannot have imagined, however, that almost 400 years later Shakespeare's words would be read and performed in countries unknown to sixteenth- and seventeenth-century England and accessed through electronic media that communicate even faster than Robin Goodfellow's "girdle round the earth in 40 minutes". Different ages have recognized different strengths and skills in Shakespeare's work: his plays have been appreciated, in Hamlet's words, for their capacity to "hold… the mirror up to nature" in the creation of character; many find Shakespeare's memorable and original use of language his most remarkable skill; others have pointed to the timeless quality of the narratives, and it is the plots which have crossed cultures to transfer so successfully into films, ballets, operas, musicals and cartoons. I was recently sent a postcard from a colleague in Australia: a picture of a koala, eyes closed and chewing a eucalyptus leaf, that had the caption "'To eat or to sleep, that is the question', William Shakesbear" – a fine example of the distance that Hamlet, and Shakespeare, has travelled.

Different ages, too, have sought to account for Shakespeare's dominance and endurance using their own cultural preoccupations: he has been praised as a "natural genius", upheld as the representative figure of English cultural superiority (the "national poet"), interrogated as a source of commercial capital, explored as a site of special – almost mystical – meaning and appropriated to support a range of political positions. Academics have subjected the works to a remarkable variety of theoretical readings: new and old historicism, feminism, Marxism, formalism, structuralism, psychoanalysis, cultural materialism and so on. *The Treasures of William Shakespeare: The Life, The Works, The Performances* is less concerned with the "why" of the Shakespeare phenomenon or an analysis of its causes and effects than with providing an illustrated and documented chronological record of his life and work, beginning in sixteenth-century Stratford and London and progressing to the present day, charting developments in performance and proliferation over the ages and throughout the world.

Shakespeare has inspired artists as diverse as William Blake and Pablo Picasso and influenced the fiction of Jane Austen, Anton Chekhov, Charles Dickens, Henrik Ibsen, Wole Soyinke and Oscar Wilde among many other great figures. Sigmund Freud and Karl Marx wrote about Shakespeare and Winston Churchill quoted him. But for most people with an interest in Shakespeare, "the play's the thing" (to borrow *Hamlet* again) and much of this book is concerned with performance. It draws extensively on the work of the Royal Shakespeare Company, the unique group of actors, directors and practitioners, whose high quality productions, education and outreach activity aim to "keep modern audiences in touch with Shakespeare as our contemporary".

Catherine M. S. Alexander

BELOW *A ninteenth-century frieze, attributed to the Irish artist Daniel Maclise, of some of Shakespeare's characters. Among them are Hamlet, Tamora, Queen of the Goths, Bottom (with ass's head) and Titania, Petruccio and Katherine, Romeo and Juliet, Juliet's Nurse, Falstaff, and Desdemona and Othello.*

The Elizabethan Age

THE COURT

Elizabeth I came to the throne at a time of great turmoil. Her father, Henry VIII, had broken from the Roman Catholic Church, largely so that he could marry Ann Boleyn, Elizabeth's mother. His son and successor, Edward VI, progressed Protestantism rigorously, but died young and was succeeded by his half sister Mary, who attempted, often with great cruelty, to restore Catholicism.

Elizabeth, a Protestant, needed to calm the situation down, establish a religious peace and create public confidence in her ability to govern the country. A skilful politician, one of her weapons was a theatrical exaggeration of her own persona.

From her coronation in 1558 onwards Queen Elizabeth was a remarkably theatrical monarch. She responded verbally to the five pageants presented by Londoners as part of her progress from the Tower of London to the ceremony, so that they became, uniquely, a series of dialogues between Queen and performers that was recorded like a play text. The coronation itself was performed on a raised stage in Westminster Abbey actually called "the theatre". But the height of her skill as a performer came 30 years later in the speech to her troops at Tilbury on 9 August 1588 – a magnificent soliloquy, in the face of the threat from the Spanish Armada:

"Wherefore I am come among you at this time but for my recreation and pleasure, being resolved in the midst and heat of the battle to live and die amongst you all, to lay down for my God and my kingdom and for my people mine honour and my blood even in the dust. I know I have the body but of a weak and feeble woman, but I have the heart and stomach of a king and a king of England too."

Elizabeth undoubtedly understood the importance of non-verbal visual display in projecting royal majesty, and as her reign progressed, with all its difficulties of religious and political dissent, she and her ministers manipulated her image, particularly in portraiture, for propaganda purposes. Costume, lighting, sets, props and emblems were carefully employed to demonstrate her wisdom, power and singularity. Protestant refugees from France and the Netherlands, such as Joris Hoefnagel and Lucas de Heere, painted her as their religious saviour, reinforcing the image on the title page of the Bishops' Bible of 1569. The iconography of Nicholas Hilliard's famous portraits of the 1570s – one has Elizabeth wearing a pelican pendant (symbolizing her selfless relationship with her subjects

TOP *Elizabeth's double-sided Great Seal, engraved by Nicholas Hilliard, was used on important public documents. The front shows the Queen holding a sceptre and orb, symbols of royal power, and on the reverse she is on horseback riding across a field of flowers.*

ABOVE *In Nicholas Hilliard's Pelican Portrait the magnificently dressed Queen, with cherries above her right ear to indicate chastity, wears a pelican pendant to demonstrate how she selflessly nurtures her nation.*

RIGHT *With the Spanish Armada gathering force in the background, the Queen rallies her troops at Tilbury.*

PANEL ABOVE RIGHT *Nicholas Hilliard was responsible for some of the most influential images of the Queen.*

PANEL BACKGROUND *Part of Robert Peake's painting from c.1601 of Queen Elizabeth I in procession.*

ABOVE *Nicholas Hilliard's miniature shows the Queen, a talented musician, playing the lute.*

NICHOLAS HILLIARD
c.1547–1618/19

Although Elizabeth never appointed an official court painter, Hilliard was associated with Queen Elizabeth I from his first portrait of her in 1572. He was a fine goldsmith as well as a miniaturist and produced jewels and a locket adorned with her image. The precision – the carefully crafted skill of his work and the symbolic imagery that he employed, which he described in his treatise *The Arte of Limning, c.*1600 – has been compared with the art that Shakespeare demonstrated in his sonnets.

(the pelican drew blood from its own breast to succour its young) and the other with a phoenix pendant (representing a person unique and chaste as well as the endurance of an hereditary monarchy) – was extended to larger domains, such as John Lumley's gardens at Nonsuch in Surrey, where the symbols were given concrete form as temples, statuary and topiary animals. Images were crafted on medals and pendants and the fashion for wearing the Queen's portrait became almost cult-like.

Equally theatrical were the lavish entertainments provided by her courtiers. In 1575, her favourite, Robert Dudley, Earl of Leicester, presented a series of masques and pageants, which included remarkable aquatic effects and lasted for 18 days, at his castle at Kenilworth, only 12 miles from Stratford. It has been suggested that Shakespeare's father may have taken him to the event and that references to the presentation of Arion in the extravagant water pageant may be found in *A Midsummer Night's Dream* (Act 2, Scene 1) and *Twelfth Night* (Act 1, Scene 2).

Until 1591 it was Elizabeth's own playing company, the Queen's Men, who dominated performances in London and the court, but subsequently the major patrons of the theatre were her senior officials – from 1594 the Lord Chamberlain's Men (who included Shakespeare) and the Lord Admiral's Men were the major performers. While it may be assumed that many of Shakespeare's plays were presented for the Queen, the only surviving court record is of a performance of *Love's Labour's Lost* in 1598. *As You Like It* may have received a royal performance in 1599 and the title page of the 1602 quarto of *The Merry Wives of Windsor* indicates that the play was performed for the Queen. A legend that first surfaced in the early eighteenth century suggests that the play was written at royal command because Elizabeth wished to see more of Falstaff – and to see him in love.

Equally conjectural, but rather appealing, is the suggestion that some of Shakespeare's witty, powerful heroines, such as Beatrice, reflect the Queen's theatrical personality.

Shakespeare's *Henry VIII*, written around 1613, concludes with the christening of the infant Elizabeth I. Thomas Cranmer, the Archbishop of Canterbury, glowingly predicts her glorious future (using the phoenix image again), and speaks of her death:

> "But she must die –
> She must, the saints must have her – yet a virgin,
> A most unspotted lily shall she pass
> To th' ground, and all the world shall mourn her."
> (Act 5, Scene 4)

Shakespeare may well have witnessed the "mourning" that he described at Elizabeth's funeral in London on 28 April 1603. The formal procession of over 1,000 mourners accompanying the coffin and a costumed effigy of the Queen was the final theatrical act of this most theatrical monarch, and was watched by an audience of tens of thousands of Londoners.

ABOVE LEFT *The Queen watches the lavish entertainments devised by Robert Dudley, Earl of Leicester, at Kenilworth Castle in 1575.*

BACKGROUND *The gardens at Nonsuch in Surrey were laid out as an allegorical compliment to the Queen's virtues.*

PANEL RIGHT *Robert Dudley, Earl of Leicester, is shown as a Knight of the Order of the Garter, an honour he received from the Queen in 1559.*

BELOW *Elizabeth's funeral procession. Her bodyguards have their pole-axes pointing downwards and the barons and earls display banners showing the emblems of Wales, England, France and the Tudors.*

Dudley's popularity with the Queen is evident in the Earldom and lands that she gifted him and in his position as one of her senior Councillors. Often described as one of Elizabeth's suitors, he was as interested in the arts as in politics and was patron of his own group of players – Leicester's Men – who performed in Stratford in the 1570s and '80s. Some of Leicester's Men eventually formed the Queen's Men.

The Elizabethan Age

THE COUNTRY

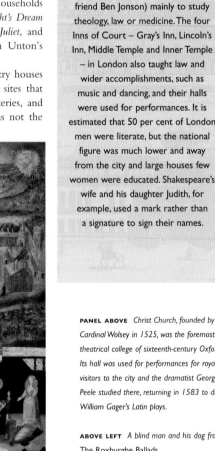

The political and religious complexities of the period required careful management by experienced personnel. One such court professional was Shakespeare's contemporary, Sir Henry Unton, who was twice Queen Elizabeth's Ambassador in France. His life was recorded in a picture commissioned at his death by his widow, Lady Dorothy, and while the image itself is unique, it records many features typical of the life of a well-connected, titled gentleman.

Clearly shown are the rich circumstances of his birth; his education at Oriel College, Oxford; travelling with his tutor in Italy; life in his country house at Wadley, near Faringdon, where he is seen studying, making music, enjoying a banquet and a masque; at war in the Netherlands and finally his death in France, the return of his body to England and the lavish funeral.

A household such as Wadley was largely self-supporting with its own brewery, dairy, bakery, buttery, armoury and specialist larders in addition to the barns and stabling on the estate. There is some indication in the picture of the staff

required to support such a lifestyle – the "middling sort" who were servants, stewards, nurses and musicians – the characters who people Shakespeare's plays. The households of *Twelfth Night*, the masques of *A Midsummer Night's Dream* and *Love's Labour's Lost*, the nurse of *Romeo and Juliet*, and the servants from a range of dramas come from Unton's stratified world.

It was during this period that many large country houses like Sir Henry's were frequently built, on prime sites that had been vacated at the dissolution of the monasteries, and were richly furnished and decorated. But this was not the

In *2 Henry IV*, Justice Shallow's young cousin William is to progress from university to an Inn of Court, an educational experience that parallels Sir Henry Unton's. Young gentlemen went to one of the universities – Oxford or Cambridge – when they were 15 or 16 (like Christopher Marlowe, but not Shakespeare or his friend Ben Jonson) mainly to study theology, law or medicine. The four Inns of Court – Gray's Inn, Lincoln's Inn, Middle Temple and Inner Temple – in London also taught law and wider accomplishments, such as music and dancing, and their halls were used for performances. It is estimated that 50 per cent of London men were literate, but the national figure was much lower and away from the city and large houses few women were educated. Shakespeare's wife and his daughter Judith, for example, used a mark rather than a signature to sign their names.

PANEL ABOVE *Christ Church, founded by Cardinal Wolsey in 1525, was the foremost theatrical college of sixteenth-century Oxford. Its hall was used for performances for royal visitors to the city and the dramatist George Peele studied there, returning in 1583 to direct William Gager's Latin plays.*

ABOVE LEFT *A blind man and his dog from The Roxburghe Ballads.*

LEFT *The unique memorial picture of Sir Henry Unton showing his life from birth to burial.*

Many popular pastimes of the period are evident in Shakespeare's plays: the hunting in *As You Like It*, the falconry that provides the "taming" analogies of *Shrew*, and the fencing that is essential to the tragic plot of *Romeo and Juliet* or used comedically in *The Merry Wives of Windsor*. More common activities, shared by women and children, were the feasting, drinking, dancing and music that occur throughout the canon, often in codified forms, and marked the church, civic and farming calendars.

RIGHT *As this woodcut shows, hunting was a very popular rural pursuit and also a good source of food.*

BOTTOM RIGHT *Harvesting was an important part of the rural calendar and often an opportunity for courting.*

PANEL RIGHT *In this woodcut, also from The Roxburghe Ballads, a family is shown enjoying the feasting that frequently occurred throughout Shakespeare's plays.*

BACKGROUND *Farm labourers clear the soil and prepare it for planting.*

experience of many. It was a period of significant social differentiation and, put simply, the rich were getting richer and the poor were getting poorer at a faster rate than ever before. Eighty or so miles away from the city and the court of London, and north of Sir Henry's estates in Wadley, life in Stratford in the heart of the Midlands was very different, as indeed it was for the majority – perhaps as much as 90 per cent of the population – who were country dwellers and workers.

The countryside around villages and towns would be unrecognizable today. Before the enclosures that created parcels of privately owned land it was characterized by great, open, unhedged fields and common pastures. Before the mechanization of agriculture, whole families and communities worked in the fields. The pattern of their working day was regulated by the sun (the hours of daylight); their working year by the church, with 23 designated feast days ("holy" days) and additional breaks at Easter, Whitsun and Christmas. Most importantly, life was regulated by and dependent on the farming year, with poor harvests and disease adding problems of famine and poverty to work that was already physically arduous. These country communities were largely self-sufficient, with the manufacturing of textiles and household goods still being carried out on a domestic basis rather than as larger scale industrial activities.

Some elements of this agricultural life, where sheep outnumbered people by three to one, may be seen in the "pastoral" scenes of *The Winter's Tale* and the Arden scenes in *As You Like It*, the former celebrating country life with sheep-shearing feasts and the latter, while humorous and romantic, well aware of the dangers and threats to rural livelihoods. The shepherd Corin's description of his rural life, in response to the goading of the court-dweller Touchstone, was typical of many:

"Sir, I am a true labourer. I earn that I eat, get that I wear; owe no man hate, envy no man's happiness; glad of other men's good, content with my harm; and the greatest of my pride is to see my ewe's graze and my lamb's suck."
(Act 3, Scene 2)

While writing his plays in the city Shakespeare was nevertheless reflecting the experiences of the majority who, like him, had grown up in rural rather than urban England.

Elizabethan Stratford

When the antiquary John Leland visited Warwickshire in the 1540s he travelled south from Warwick to Barford and Charlecote, following the course of the river Avon, and then arrived in Stratford, which he described carefully:

"The town of Stratford occupies a level site on the right bank or side of the Avon, as one goes downstream. It has two or three very large streets, and back lanes besides. Of the main streets one leads from east to west and another from south to north. The buildings are timber, and of reasonable quality. The town belongs to the Bishop of Worcester. On Holy Rood Day, 14 September, each year a great fair is held. The large parish church, which stands at the south end of the town, is a fine piece of architecture."

Hugh Clopton, Lord Mayor of London in 1491, built Stratford's grandest house, New Place, which Shakespeare bought in 1597. Shakespeare's father, John, was a tenant of land owned by Sir William Clopton in Hampton Lucy. Clopton House, the family home on the outskirts of Stratford, was used as a base by Ambrose Rookwood, one of the Gunpowder Plot conspirators in 1605. He was eventually captured and executed.

Then he listed the most imposing features of the town: the Trinity (more accurately the Guild) Chapel that was built by Hugh Clopton, a Lord Mayor of London; Clopton's grand house; the grammar school on the south side of the Chapel that was established by Thomas Jolliffe, a university teacher born in Stratford; the alms houses and the bridge across the Avon that was also built by Hugh Clopton. So it was a small town with some distinguished buildings and some distinguished inhabitants. There were about 200 families in all – a population of perhaps 1,000 people – although it is difficult to be precise at this period. There was a general move from country to town, but disease was prevalent: it is estimated that 10 per cent of Stratford's inhabitants died of flu or typhus in 1558–9, and about 16 per cent died of the plague in 1564, the year of Shakespeare's birth. In the whole of England, there were about three million people, fewer than there had been before the Black Death 200 years before, but the population was just beginning to grow and more children were surviving the perils of infancy.

The Avon was an important part of Stratford's prosperity. Leland wrote that until Clopton built his stone bridge "there was only a poor wooden bridge with no causeway leading up to it. Consequently many poor people and others refused to visit Stratford when the Avon was in spate, or if they did come they had to risk their lives". Travelling east and west had always been possible on the river, connecting all the way to the port of Bristol in the west, but was less easy going north to south. After the new bridge was built, Stratford became an important post on the route that transported salt from Cheshire to London. So the small town became the centre for trades, such as tailoring, shoemaking, carpentry and blacksmithing, and markets that served local villages, and began to acquire a national significance. It lacked the prominence of the ancient cities of Coventry to the north or Oxford to the south, but still had regular contacts with the capital.

The Avon bisects Warwickshire into two distinct areas. North of the river was the area known as Arden, the hillier, wooded part of the county and perhaps the setting for *As You Like It*. In Shakespeare's day, it had a reputation as a rather dangerous or suspect place: there were wild animals, rumours of bandits or outlaws, and it was also where some of the Catholic, recusant families hid out. Nearby, Baddesley Clinton had "priest-holes" to hide its Catholic celebrants and Coughton Court was heavily implicated in the Gunpowder Plot (in fact, the main conspirators of 1605 – Catesby, Tresham and Winter – all had Stratford connections).

ABOVE *Baddesley Clinton, to the north of Stratford, still has three priest-holes where Catholics hid from persecution.*

BELOW *The Clopton Bridge, over the Avon, improved travel and contributed to the prosperity of Stratford.*

PANEL ABOVE RIGHT *Hugh Clopton, who came from a prominent Stratford family, is remembered in stained glass as a benefactor of the Guild Chapel.*

BACKGROUND *The house in Henley Street where William Shakespeare was born.*

JOHN LELAND
1506–52

In the 1530s and '40s, Henry VIII's library keeper and antiquary, John Leland, undertook a research tour throughout England, which he planned to form the basis of a great original work, *Histories and Antiquities of this Nation*. Although he never completed the work, his notes formed the basis of *Leland's Itinerary*, which was published in Oxford in 1710 and provides some of the earliest descriptions of Tudor England.

South of the river was Felden, a flatter and more prosperous, fertile area where agriculture benefited from the Avon's regular flooding. Predominantly Protestant, wealthy, landowning families had homes in this area and it was here that the grain, the basis of Stratford's successful malting and brewing industry, was grown.

The 1553 Charter of Incorporation established the administration of Stratford, creating a Corporation of aldermen and burgesses – largely the senior tradesmen – whose responsibilities included the grammar school and the Guild Chapel. In 1564, the Corporation ordered the defacement of images in the Chapel, probably to demonstrate the Protestant allegiance of the town.

This was the year of Shakespeare's birth – in a small market town in the Midlands not in itself of great significance yet nonetheless reflecting national events.

ABOVE *A nineteenth-century view of Shakespeare's school (King Edward VI's Grammar School) with the Guild Chapel to its left.*

LEFT *Holy Trinity Church where William Shakespeare was baptised in 1564 and buried in 1616.*

BELOW *The gatehouse of Coughton Court where, on 5 November 1605, Sir Everard Digby and Jesuit priests waited for news of the Gunpowder Plot.*

Shakespeare in Stratford

William Shakespeare, the third of eight children and the first boy, was born in 1564 and baptised on 26 April in Holy Trinity Church. His birthday is traditionally set three days earlier, assuming the usual delay between birth and baptism. April 23 is also, conveniently, St George's Day, thus creating a patriotic elision between national saint and national playwright.

His mother, Mary Arden, was from a prosperous farming family at Wilmcote, a village just outside Stratford, and his father, John, was a glover, tanner and wool-dealer in the town. John was also a member of the Corporation, becoming Bailiff (the equivalent of Mayor) in 1568. It was while he held this office, which included the responsibility for licensing visiting actors, that the Queen's Men and Worcester's Men performed in Stratford for the first time.

John Shakespeare's position would also have enabled William to attend the grammar school, probably when he was about eight, having first gone to a "petty school" for his basic education. At the King's New School, he would have learned Latin, encountered classical plays and stories and learnt to write letters, speeches and arguments. The scene in *The Merry Wives of Windsor*, when the young William recites his Latin lesson, may well reflect personal experience.

The family home in Henley Street (now known as Shakespeare's Birthplace) was also the centre of his father's business with workshops on the ground floor for preparing and working animal skins. The hygienic disposal of domestic and commercial waste was frequently a problem at this time and records show that John was fined for making a dunghill in the street rather than using the authorized facilities.

ABOVE *Shakespeare's father, John, wearing his robes of office and standing in front of his house in Henley Street (Shakespeare's birthplace), is remembered in stained glass in the Guild Chapel.*

RIGHT *"Hewlands", now known as Anne Hathaway's Cottage, was the childhood home of Shakespeare's wife.*

EDMOND
SHAKESPEARE
DIED DECEMBER
1607.

SHAKESPEARE'S SEVEN BROTHERS
AND SISTERS

Joan 1558–?60
Margaret 1562–3
Gilbert 1566–1612
(became a haberdasher)
Joan, 1569–1646 (survived her
husband, William Hart, a hatter,
by 30 years and lived in the
"Birthplace" in Henley Street)
Ann, 1571–9
Richard 1574–1613
Edmond 1580–1607
(an actor who was buried in
Southwark, where there
is a fine memorial in
the Cathedral)

John Shakespeare, held many offices under council & served as Bailiff & Justice of the Peace

SIR FRANCIS BACON
1561–1626
A prominent statesman and lawyer. The dates work, but nothing about the style of his essays and other writings is at all like Shakespeare's plays.

CHRISTOPHER MARLOWE
1564–93
A great playwright, but his well-documented murder surely prevented him writing the bulk of the Shakespeare canon.

THE EARL OF OXFORD,
1550–1604
As with Marlowe, the date of his death precludes Oxford from the authorship of plays that can be dated, with certainty, later in the reign of King James. The same argument, of course, can be applied to Queen Elizabeth I.

OPPOSITE PAGE PANEL *The memorial tablet to Shakespeare's actor brother Edmond that can be found in Southwark Cathedral.*

RIGHT *Charlecote Park was the home of the Lucy family. The house that still stands today was built by Sir Thomas Lucy in 1551. Legend suggests that Shakespeare was caught poaching deer in the grounds.*

It is likely that Shakespeare left school when he was 15, and perhaps he then helped in his father's business, but it is the absence of evidence during this period – sometimes called "the lost years" – that has contributed to a number of myths and controversies. It has been suggested that he worked as a schoolmaster in the country, that he was with a Catholic family in Lancashire, that he had joined an acting company or travelled abroad, and that he had to leave Stratford in a hurry having been caught deer-poaching in Charlecote Park. He was, however, back in town in November 1582. On 27 November, a licence from the Bishop of Worcester permitted his marriage and was followed by a special bond the next day. There is some confusion or even irregularity here: Anne is named "Whately" rather than "Hathaway" in the licence that also allowed a speedy marriage after just one reading of the banns. The wrong name may be a simple error, while the haste may reflect the fact that Anne Hathaway (born in 1555 or '56, and one of seven children from a farming family in Shottery just outside Stratford) was pregnant. Shakespeare, at 18, was technically a minor and Anne was eight years older. Their daughter Susanna was born in May the following year and their twins, Judith and Hamnet, early in 1585.

Despite the quantity of contemporary evidence that Shakespeare wrote his plays, it is the lack of hard information about the missing years, coupled with the apparent ordinariness of his life, that has fuelled the controversy about authorship. A desire to make the playwright exceptional, preferably metropolitan and upper class or, at the very least, university educated, has led some to propose a vast conspiracy and suggest alternative authors for the plays: Sir Francis Bacon, Christopher Marlowe, the 17th Earl of Oxford and even Queen Elizabeth I. Such claims tend to reveal more about the proposers of these theories than they do about Shakespeare.

Shakespeare's London

The writer Robert Greene's famously disparaging reference to Shakespeare as "the upstart crow" in *A Groatsworth of Wit* helps place the playwright firmly in London by 1592, but it is likely that he had arrived a couple of years earlier and while he would eventually perform at court it was not the city of the royal palaces of Westminster, Whitehall and St James that he first encountered.

ABOVE *William Herbert, 3rd Earl of Pembroke, was an important patron of Shakespeare and possibly the "Mr W. H." to whom the Sonnets are dedicated.*

BELOW *An arena for cockfighting: the observers are betting on the outcome of the fight.*

BELOW RIGHT *"Wedding at Horsleydown in Bermondsey" by the Antwerp-born Joris Hoefnagel (1542–1600) shows marriage celebrations in what is now part of south-east London.*

He lived and worked on the south bank of the Thames in the Liberty of the Clink. The Liberties were a curious administrative anomaly: once monastic lands, at the Dissolution of the Monasteries under Henry VIII, they ceased to have any clear jurisdiction and remained free of the control of the civil authorities. They became the city's playgrounds, areas of somewhat dubious reputation, and the site of hundreds of inns, bowling alleys, pits for bull-baiting, bear-baiting and cockfighting, brothels and purpose-built theatres. The south bank area also contained the prisons and the smelliest trades – tanning, soap-making and brewing.

The whole city was busy and growing fast; it was crowded and frequently unruly. The original walled city, with its Westminster power base, was filling up and overspilling with vagrants, vagabonds, former soldiers and sailors, discharged servants, orphans and refugees. There were frequent attempts at population control, including restrictions on new building and the conversion of old buildings into tenement dwellings. Shortages of fuel, bread and water, and outbreaks of bubonic plague, added to the tension, but at the same time life was exciting and, for some, prosperous. The trade by river and sea was the basis of the city's growth and attracted merchants (the founding of Gresham's Royal Exchange both regulated and made their transactions more secure). In the taverns, travellers told tales not only of Europe, but also of Russia, Turkey and the New World. A small group of Italians lived in the city and there was also a black presence – mainly servants and entertainers, but sizeable enough for the Queen to express her displeasure and for plans of repatriation to be considered. Aspiring politicians and artists, keen for royal patronage and social and economic advancement, were drawn to the city and the court, as were many young noblemen hoping to catch the Queen's attention through their own patronage of the arts.

Shakespeare's dedication of his long poems *Venus and Adonis* and *The Rape of Lucrece* to Henry Wriothesley, the Earl of Southampton, suggests the identity of his first patron. Southampton was well born and rich, and it was

ROBERT GREENE
c.1560–92

Greene was a proficient writer in many styles and genres, with a colourful private life, who may have collaborated with Shakespeare on the early *Henry VI* plays. His prose work *Pandosto* is the source story for *The Winter's Tale*, although it has an element of incest that is more salacious than in Shakespeare's play. His autobiographical writings tell of London's lowlife and he was said by his contemporary, Gabriel Harvey, to have died from a surfeit of pickled herrings and Rhenish wine.

LEFT *Thomas Nashe (1567–c.1601), was frequently in trouble with the church and best remembered for his prose writing.*

Thomas Nashe

BELOW *John Florio also benefited from the Earl of Southampton's patronage. He owned a famous library and translated Montaigne's Essays.*

HENRY WRIOTHESLEY,
EARL OF SOUTHAMPTON
1573–1624

known that, as an orphan, he stood to inherit a large fortune when he came of age. Writers were queuing up for his patronage and, a keen theatre-goer, he supported Barnes, John Florio and Thomas Nashe as well as Shakespeare. The dedication of the First Folio of Shakespeare's works to the Herbert brothers (William and Philip, the 3rd and 4th Earls of Pembroke respectively), who were both known as generous patrons, suggests that Shakespeare received further support from them. What is certain, however, is that by 1594 Shakespeare had new connections. Henry Carey, the first Baron Hunsdon and the then Lord Chamberlain, set up two new playing companies, largely as an attempt to regulate stage performances. One, his own Lord Chamberlain's Men, was to perform at the Theatre and the other, the Lord Admiral's Men (headed by his son-in-law, Charles Howard) at the Rose. Shakespeare, already known as an actor and an established playwright, was, with other actor-sharers such as Richard Burbage and Will Kempe, a founder member of the Lord Chamberlain's Men and remained with the company for the rest of his working life. They moved to the Globe theatre in 1599, and after Elizabeth's death in 1603 the new monarch, King James, became their patron and their name changed to the King's Men.

OPPOSITE PAGE PANEL *Robert Greene was notorious for his behaviour and appearance as well as his writing. In this posthumously published picture he is shown in his winding sheet, still writing after death.*

PANEL RIGHT *Shakespeare's patron, the Earl of Southampton, was painted many times, frequently with long hair, for which he was famous, carefully arranged over his shoulders. He is seen here, imprisoned in the Tower, with his cat.*

LEFT *Philip Herbert, 4th Earl of Pembroke, like his brother William (opposite) was a great patron of the arts. The First Folio is dedicated to them both.*

BACKGROUND *A map of the Cities of London and Westminster, drawn in 1563 by William Darton.*

Southampton allied himself to the Earl of Essex's insurrection in 1601, paying Shakespeare's company 40 shillings to perform *Richard II*, a play that depicts the successful usurpation of a monarch. When the rebellion failed, Essex was executed and Southampton jailed for life and stripped of his titles, but he was released and rehabilitated when James came to the throne in 1603. He is sometimes proposed as the young man to whom the first of Shakespeare's sonnets are addressed.

Shakespeare's Contemporaries

It does a disservice to the writers of the Elizabethan age to identify them simply as Shakespeare's contemporaries and in some way just an adjunct to the Great Man. In this remarkable period of literary talent, there were dramatists, poets and prose writers who were as prolific and as skilled as Shakespeare and whose reputations equalled or exceeded his. Of this group of eminent writers, the lives of the following individuals can be connected most explicitly with Shakespeare's. He may also have borrowed or adapted their work, which was quite normal for the time.

BELOW *Ben Jonson's cross section of London life gather in Smithfield for Bartholomew Fair in the RSC's 1969 production with Helen Mirren (left) as Doll Tearsheet.*

BELOW RIGHT *Shakespeare's friend Michael Drayton in an eighteenth-century engraving that has awarded him the laurel crown of a great poet.*

THOMAS LODGE (?1557–1625)

Shakespeare's source for *As You Like It* was the hugely popular prose romance *Rosalynde* by Thomas Lodge that was published in 1590. Lodge was one of the influential "University Wits" (Lodge, Lyly and Peele from Oxford; Greene, Marlowe and Nash from Cambridge) who are credited with the introduction of a sophisticated, versatile style of drama during the 1590s. Shakespeare's addition of the characters Touchstone, Corin and Jaques to Lodge's pastoral plot gives the play a tougher, contemporary edge as well as comedic range.

MICHAEL DRAYTON (1563–1631)

Drayton's life overlaps with Shakespeare's in a number of tantalizing ways. Their backgrounds were similar: Drayton was also born in Warwickshire, in Hartshill, and was the son of a butcher. He stayed regularly with Lady Rainsford, the daughter of his former patron, at Clifford Chambers, just south of Stratford-upon-Avon, where his medical needs were met by John Hall, Shakespeare's son-in-law. Legend identifies Drayton and Shakespeare as drinking buddies. Best known as a professional poet, he also wrote plays for the Admiral's Men – the only one that survives, *Sir John Oldcastle*, was wrongly attributed to Shakespeare in 1619. His greatest work, the topographical verse tour of Britain, *Poly-Olbion*, includes a description of the Forest of Arden as it is encroached by enclosures and buildings.

The Spanish Tragedie
OR
Hieronimo is mad againe.

Containing the lamentable end of Don Horatio, and
Bel-imperia; with the pittifull death of Hieronimo.

Newly corrected, amended, and enlarged with new
Additions of the Painters part, and others, as
it hath of late been divers times acted.

LONDON,
Printed by W. White, and are to be sold by I. White
and T. Langley at their Shop over against the
Sarazens head without New-gate. 1615

FAR LEFT *The original title page of Thomas Kyd's play The Spanish Tragedy.*

LEFT *Ben Jonson was honoured by burial in Westminster Abbey, where the inscription on his tombstone, "O rare Ben Jonson", reflects the respect and affection of his contemporaries.*

BELOW *Christopher Marlowe: some believe that had he lived he might have outmatched Shakespeare in range and skill.*

BACKGROUND *Avaricious legacy hunters gather at the bedside of the wealthy Volpone in the RSC's 1999 production of Ben Jonson's satire on Jacobean London.*

THOMAS KYD (1558–94)

While less is known of Kyd's life than of his contemporaries', his influence is clear. He is thought to have written a play called *Hamlet* (known now as the "ur-Hamlet"), which although lost is reckoned to be a source for Shakespeare's play. Shakespeare may have been responding, too, to Kyd's *The Spanish Tragedy* of 1592, the most popular play of the period, when he incorporated revenge, a ghost, delay, madness, a range of deaths (including a consideration of suicide) and a "play within a play" into his great work. In 1593, Kyd was imprisoned and tortured, dying soon after his release, and in 1602 (perhaps in response to the popularity of the new play, Shakespeare's *Hamlet*) Ben Jonson was employed to write additional "mad" scenes for *The Spanish Tragedy*.

Ben Jonson

BEN JONSON (1572–1637)

Brought up by his stepfather, a master builder, Jonson was apprenticed to a bricklayer, but left the work to become a soldier fighting in The Netherlands. On his return, he became an actor (like Shakespeare) and began writing plays for the theatre builder and owner Philip Henslowe. Unlike Shakespeare, the setting and plots for Jonson's popular comedies – *Every Man in his Humour*, *Every Man Out of His Humour*, *Volpone*, *Epicoene*, *The Alchemist* and *Bartholomew Fair* – were contemporary city life, but he had a great range and the court masques that he wrote for King James were imaginative and sophisticated.

The respect that Jonson had for Shakespeare and the friendship between the two men is evidenced in his great memorial verse "To the memory of my beloved, the author Mr William Shakespeare: and what he hath left us" in the introductory material of the First Folio. Shakespeare is "the applause, the delight, the wonder of our stage… He was not of an age but for all time", and it is in this verse that for the first time he is called "Sweet swan of Avon".

CHRISTOPHER MARLOWE (1564–93)

Marlowe's life has excited as much speculation and controversy as Shakespeare's and their early lives were similar. Born in Canterbury to the son of a shoemaker and freeman of the city, Marlowe attended the King's School and in 1580 went to Corpus Christi College, Cambridge on a scholarship. His subsequent life and career is less clear: he was certainly a soldier, probably a counterfeiter, spy and murderer, possibly a heretic, and was stabbed to death in a brawl in a Deptford tavern in 1593. It is clear that from the late 1580s he was writing some of the greatest plays in the English language – *Tamburlaine*, *Doctor Faustus*, *The Jew of Malta*, *Edward II* and *The Massacre at Paris* – that influenced Shakespeare's *Titus Andronicus*, *Richard II* and *The Merchant of Venice*. Like Shakespeare, he drew on Ovid particularly in his narrative poem *Hero and Leander*, which is similar to Shakespeare's *Venus and Adonis*, and Shakespeare quotes the poem directly in Phoebe's speech in *As You Like It* (Act 3, Scene 5).

The Elizabethan Stage

Plays were commonly performed in open spaces, such as market places and inn yards like the Saracen's Head in Islington and the Boar's Head in Aldgate, until the first purpose built public theatre, the Red Lion, was opened in Stepney (the area now known as the East End of London) in 1567.

ABOVE *The Globe, Shakespeare's theatre, was situated on the south bank of the Thames in the Londoners' entertainment area.*

PANEL RIGHT *The characteristic circular, arena-style shape of the theatres is shown here in a 1614 engraving of the Swan.*

BELOW *Hamlet, here in Eugene Delacroix's painting of 1855, discovers he has murdered Polonius, who was eavesdropping behind a curtain. A curtain covered the "disclosing space" at the back of the Elizabethan stage.*

While records indentify the businessmen, such as Philip Henslowe, who built and owned the new theatres and, to a lesser extent, the actors who performed in them, there is limited evidence about their size, shape and capacity, or the style of performances that took place there. Until the remains of the Rose Theatre were discovered in 1989, followed shortly by the foundations of the Globe, almost the only resource was the sketch of the Swan made by a Dutch visitor, Johannes de Witt, in about 1596 and copied by his friend Aernout van Buchel.

The stage, probably about 1.7 m (5 ft) high, projected into the almost circular theatre with the "groundlings", who paid 1d admission, standing on three sides and the rest of the audience, who paid 3d, seated in three tiers of wooden seating. Two doors at the rear of the stage provided entrances and exits for the actors and there is likely to have been an area between the doors – the curtained disclosing space – that may have been an additional acting space or a store. Polonius may have been murdered behind the arras here or Desdemona's bed revealed. Above the stage was a gallery, but its purpose is uncertain. Some suggest that it was an audience seating area, some that it was a musicians' gallery, others that it was part of the performance space. The de Witt sketch of the Swan shows a figure above the canopy over the stage: perhaps he is touting for custom ("Roll up, roll up!") or he may be part of the action. Stage directions in 1 *Henry IV* and *The Tempest* indicate that a character appears "on the top". The area beneath the stage, accessed by a trap, provided an additional entrance – for the ghost in *Hamlet*, say – or an exit for a descent into hell.

The stage was bare, although the pillars supporting the canopy afforded two potential hiding, spying or overhearing places. Furniture was sparse, probably little more than a bench, chairs or a throne and the plays needed very little in the way of stage properties. Costume, on the other hand, was lavish and very expensive. Dress conveyed status and reflected Elizabethan sumptuary laws; a prescriptive code that determined who was allowed to dress in specific styles, colours and fabrics. Servants who were bequeathed clothes by their masters sold them on to actors and Henslowe's accounts show that a doublet for use on stage could cost as much as £3 and a gown up to £7.

Performances took place in daylight, in the afternoon, and without the benefit of lighting effects or stage scenery it was the text – the language of the play – that had to convey time of day, location and mood. Clear identification of character was important too, particularly as one actor may have played two or three roles in a production. Audiences presumably had no difficulty with such conventions and without expectations of realism were willing to use their imagination. Shakespeare sometimes used prologues to encourage such a suspension of disbelief: the opening Chorus in *Henry V* begs "Let us… on your imaginary forces work" and, referring directly to the theatre, suggests:

LEFT *Johannes de Witt's sketch of the Swan theatre (c.1596) is important evidence of Elizabethan staging.*

PHILIP HENSLOWE
1555/6–1616

Henslowe was an important and integral figure in the Elizabethan theatre world, an impresario, associated particularly with the Admiral's Men and the Rose theatre and perhaps, therefore, in competition with Shakespeare's company. His stepdaughter, Joan, married the great actor Edward Alleyn (best known as the lead in Marlowe's *Jew of Malta*, *Tamburlaine* and *Doctor Faustus*) with whom Henslowe collaborated in theatre projects. In 1619, Alleyn founded Dulwich College that now holds their papers, including Henslowe's *Diary* (part account book, part business record) that is the most important resource of theatre practice in the period.

"Suppose within the girdles of these walls
Are now confined two mighty monarchies,
Whose high upreared and abutting fronts
The perilous narrow ocean parts asunder.
Piece out our imperfections with your thoughts."
Prologue

It is a mistake to think of the Elizabethan audience as an unsophisticated mob, ever ready to barrack or throw rotten vegetables – they were clearly discriminating listeners with well-developed imaginations.

ABOVE LEFT *Excavations of the site of the Rose theatre, which was built in 1587, revealed the size and shape of the auditorium and stage.*

ABOVE RIGHT *The excavations of the Rose enabled conjectural reconstructions of the theatre, as seen here in a sketch made in 1999.*

BELOW LEFT *The lavish costumes of the Elizabethan stage showed rank and status and are recreated here in C. Wilhelm's designs for a production of* As You Like It *in Manchester.*

BELOW RIGHT *In an innovative production, Mephistopheles (Alan Howard, left, disguised as a friar) torments Faustus (David Waller, right) with the seven deadly sins (Marlowe's* Dr Faustus, *RSC, 1970).*

Shakespeare's Texts

Playwrights of Shakespeare's period seem to have had little interest in the publication of their plays and there was certainly no sense of personal ownership or copyright in the modern sense. Plays were written primarily for performance, not publication, and were the property of the playing company who purchased them and not the individual dramatist.

Only a small proportion of the plays that were written and performed at this time actually made it into print. This may be a reflection of their poor quality or, on the other hand, an indication of the playing companies' desire to retain a monopoly of – and an audience for – their valuable commodities.

About half of Shakespeare's texts were published during his lifetime in small, single play, quarto editions. "Quarto" is the name given to a book in which the printed page has been folded twice, producing four leaves and eight pages. Some Shakespearian quartos, Quarto 1 *Romeo and Juliet* (1597), for example, and Quarto 1 *Hamlet* (1603) appear to be have been unauthorized and were quickly replaced by a second, and often significantly different, quarto – Quarto 2. The "bad" first quartos may be pirated editions of successful and popular plays, the text re-created by disloyal actors or audience members.

Shakespeare wrote his plays in longhand and delivered them to the playhouse where they would be prepared for performance. Rather than creating multiple copies of the complete text of the whole work, a lengthy and time-consuming process, it is believed that cut "cue scripts" were prepared for the actors, giving just their own lines with the appropriate speech cue. It may have been Shakespeare's handwritten copy, his "foul papers", that was eventually sent to the printers or a more detailed prompt book or a "fair copy" made by a professional scribe. The scrivener Ralph Crane prepared the scripts of *The Tempest* and *The Winter's Tale* for publication in the First Folio. No complete play manuscript survives, although some argue that a small part of the co-authored *Sir Thomas More* is in Shakespeare's handwriting.

The publisher purchased the play in manuscript form, registered his ownership in the Stationers' Register, appointed the printer and subsequently sold the volume, probably in his own bookshop. He was also responsible for clearing permission from the Master of the Revels, whose task was the licensing and censorship of plays. Some of this information is conveyed on the title pages of the quartos, but there was space there, too, for promotional material – the name of the playing company, a special royal performance, a gripping moment from the play.

In the early 1620s, John Heminges and Henry Condell, two of Shakespeare's colleagues from the King's Men, began to prepare the great memorial volume *Mr. William Shakespeare's Comedies, Histories, & Tragedies*, now better known as the First Folio (this and the subsequent seventeenth-century folios of his work are usually referred to by letter and number – F1, F2, F3). Without this work, the first book published in England devoted solely to the plays of a single dramatist,

ABOVE *The first page of The Tempest, the first play in the First Folio.*

RIGHT *The title page of the Third Quarto of Hamlet, which was printed in 1611.*

BACKGROUND *The manuscript of Sir Thomas More. It may be in Shakespeare's handwriting and can be seen in the British Library in London.*

OPPOSITE *In an Elizabethan printing house the man on the left prepares to ink the type, while his colleague operates the press.*

Shakespeare's first published works, *Venus and Adonis* and *The Rape of Lucrece*, were printed by Stratford-born Richard Field. The history plays, *Richard II, Richard III* and *1 Henry IV*, all of which went into five editions, were printed by Andrew Wise in 1597–8. A quarto print run was usually 800 copies and they sold for 6d each. The First Folio was printed by William Jaggard and his son Isaac at their printing house on the corner of Aldersgate Street and the Barbican in London. The pages for a quarto took about two weeks to print.

18 plays by Shakespeare – those not published in his lifetime – would be lost. Even so, it is not quite a Complete Works, lacking the co-authored *Pericles* and *The Two Noble Kinsmen* and the poems. It is an impressive, large volume ("folio" is the name given to a work created from sheets of paper folded just once, giving two leaves and four pages), not least because of the engraving of Shakespeare by Martin Droeshout on the title page and the commemorative verses by Ben Jonson and Hugh Holland. It is estimated that an average labourer at the time earned a shilling a day and the Folio cost £1, but nevertheless, when published in 1623, it sold sufficiently well that a second edition was produced in 1632. In 2003, Oriel College, Oxford sold its First Folio for an estimated £3.5 million.

ABOVE *The First Folio omitted the co-authored* Pericles, *seen here in this RSC production from 2002 with Kananu Kirimi as Marina (left) and Ray Fearon as Pericles (centre).*

LEFT AND BELOW *The title pages of quarto editions of* Richard II *and* Romeo and Juliet*. Both are first quartos and one,* Romeo and Juliet, *is an unauthorized "bad quarto". Both are being promoted with performance information beneath the titles.*

An enduring difficulty for editors, actors and readers is the differences between the printed versions of the plays, between the quartos and folios, and therefore in determining what Shakespeare actually wrote. Some variations are minor, single word differences that may be explained by errors or slips in the printing house, while others are more significant, suggesting, perhaps, authorial or performance revisions. It is common practice for modern scholarly editions to give minor variants in footnotes or, in the case of major differences, as in *King Lear* or *Hamlet*, to print parallel versions side by side.

"The Play's the Thing"

For many it is the range of Shakespeare's subject matter that makes him the greatest dramatist of all time. He wrote fantasy, horror, thrillers, and great love stories. He wrote ancient, medieval and contemporary history; he tackled social problems, politics and relationships. He wrote about the classical world and modern cities. He could move audiences with farce, tragedy and romance.

ABOVE *Lillie Langtry as Cleopatra in 1890: the tableaux and dances, and the scene-shifting required to create pictorial realism, led to a production that lasted four and a half hours.*

BELOW *The gravediggers from Hamlet, as seen here in this 2001 RSC production, add some humour to the tragedy.*

Different ages have recognized different skills and qualities in Shakespeare's work. From the eighteenth century onwards, and in part as a defence against the criticism that he failed to write to classical rules and models, Shakespeare was praised for his creation of character – holding a mirror up to nature. His characters have proved so memorable that they act as a shorthand for personalities or types: Romeo for a young male lover, Cleopatra for a mature female lover, Hamlet as a solitary thinker, Falstaff as a gluttonous John Bull figure, and Shylock as an all-purpose epithet for a Jew. Gradually Shakespeare's unique blending of genres – for example, incorporating the humour of the gravediggers into the tragedy of *Hamlet* or the Porter into *Macbeth* – was recognized as a strength rather than a failing.

A surprising, almost bravura, feature of Shakespeare's dramatic writing is the frequency with which he reminds the audience that it is watching a play. Allusions to boy actors (*Antony and Cleopatra*), acting (*Hamlet*), the Globe theatre (the opening chorus of *Henry V*), the use of the play within the play as a plot device (*The Mousetrap* in *Hamlet*), the employment of prologues and epilogues and frequent references to acts and scenes all suggest a confident compact between the playwright and the audience that took delight in its awareness of effect.

The most distinctive feature of Shakespeare's skill as a dramatist, however, is his sustained dexterity with language and rhetoric. Ostensibly simple and never straining for ostentatious effect, he creates memorable phrases and speeches that live beyond the worlds of the plays: to be more sinned against than sinning; to act more in sorrow than in anger; to play fast and loose; to be tongue-tied; to knit your brows, stand on ceremony, or have too much of a good thing – all were coined by Shakespeare. How much does a modern politician owe to Shakespeare's skill of presenting ideas in threes: "Some are born great, some achieve greatness, some have greatness thrust upon them"; "Friends, Romans, countrymen". Or his use of repetition: "Tomorrow and tomorrow and tomorrow", or "To be or not to be"? One of his most frequent devices is a sophisticated use of lists, sometimes deployed for serious effect as in Richard II's moving

"For God's sake let us sit upon the ground
And tell sad stories of the death of kings,
How some have been deposed, some slain in war,
Some haunted by the ghosts they have deposed,
Some poisoned by their wives, some sleeping killed,
All murdered."
(*Richard II*, Act 3, Scene 2)

RHETORIC

Rhetoric, the art of using language for persuasion particularly in speech, developed in classical times as a highly codified theory of the use of language (particularly in Aristotle's *Rhetoric* and the work of Quintilian and Cicero). From the Middle Ages onwards rhetoric was part of the *trivium* that, with logic and grammar, formed the core educational curriculum. Shakespeare would have learned the five processes of composition – invention, arrangement, style, memory and delivery – and figures of speech at Stratford's grammar school and exploited them throughout his plays most noticeably in the great set-piece speeches of John of Gaunt about England (*Richard II*, Act 2, Scene 1) and Mark Antony's funeral speech for Julius Caesar (Act 3, Scene 2).

PANEL BACKGOUND ABOVE *Mark Antony, painted here by William Holmes Sullivan, exploits his rhetorical skill as he delivers his funeral oration for Caesar.*

OPPOSITE *The off-stage audience watch the on-stage audience of Hamlet, Claudius, Gertrude and Ophelia watching the "play within a play" (The Mousetrap), from a production of Hamlet in 1958.*

or in Jaques' "seven ages of man" speech in *As You Like It*, but frequently used for comic effect, as in Touchstone's listing of the degrees of lying in the last scene of *As You Like It*.

It is often said that the Elizabethan audience went to the theatre to *hear* a play. They were undoubtedly more sophisticated listeners than today's audiences and revelled in puns and quibbles. Juliet's speech to her Nurse when she believes that Romeo is dead is a fine example frequently, alas, cut in productions that believe such language facility is beyond a teenage girl or inappropriate at a moment of high emotion:

> "What devil art thou that dost torment me thus?
> This torture should be roared in dismal hell.
> Hath Romeo slain himself? Say thou but 'Ay',
> And that bare vowel 'I' shall poison more
> Than the death-darting eye of cockatrice.
> I am not I if there be such an 'Ay',
> Or those eyes shut that makes thee answer 'Ay'.
> If he be slain, say 'ay'; or if not, 'No'.
> Brief sounds determine of my weal or woe."
> (*Romeo and Juliet* Act 3, Scene 2)

Some clever punning relies for its effect on skilled verse speaking and actors engage in intensive training for these special demands.

Peter Hall (above) founded the Royal Shakespeare Company in 1960 and worked closely with the director John Barton in establishing high standards of verse speaking and vocal training, believing that meaning and therefore effective communication between actor and audience were best achieved through the careful study of the rhythm, stresses and pauses (often indicated by the punctuation) of Shakespeare's lines. The ensemble nature of the RSC gives actors experience in a range of Shakespearian roles, and effective communication through voice remains at the heart of the company's rehearsal process, performances and work with teachers and students.

ABOVE The "seven ages of man" from "the infant,/ Mewling and puking in the nurse's arm" to "second childishness and mere oblivion,/Sans teeth, sans eyes, sans taste, sans everything" shown in the window of the Folger Shakespeare Library in Washington DC.

RIGHT Alan Howard in the title role of Richard II (RSC, 1980), a play written entirely in verse and with great formality in its use of language.

The Comedies

HAPPILY EVER AFTER

It is easy to forget that in his own time Shakespeare was one of a number of gifted writers who borrowed plots from each other and from earlier writers, such as Plautus and Ovid, and who were working within established styles and conventions. When he began to write comedies in the 1590s, the genre had a number of characteristics, some of which had very little to do with humour.

ABOVE *The programme for an evening's "amateur" entertainment at the Theatre Royal, Birmingham. It includes Charles Dickens – a great Shakespeare enthusiast – performing in* The Merry Wives of Windsor.

RIGHT *Dante, shown here with Virgil in a fourteenth-century painting, influenced the development and shape of European comedy through his* Divine Comedy.

PANEL FAR RIGHT TOP *William Kempe, the comic actor whose roles included Dogberry in* Much Ado About Nothing *and Bottom in* A Midsummer Night's Dream.

PANEL FAR RIGHT BELOW *The popular comic actor Robert Armin dressed as "John of the Hospital" in his own 1609 play,* The History of the Two Maids of More-Clacke.

From the Greek classics came the enduring association between comedy and fertility rites – sex was an important strand in this type of drama. Aristotle made the distinction that comedy was about ordinary people in everyday situations, while tragedy was the reverse (extraordinary people in unusual situations). By the time of Dante and his *Divine Comedy* (c.1310) a further distinction was emerging concerned with the structure of the plot and the direction of the narrative: comedy begins harshly, but ends happily (from misfortune to joy), while the opposite is the case with tragedy (from joy to misfortune). In England, the medieval morality play introduced farce and comic elements to support the didactic function of the drama and reinforce the Christian message. By the time of the Renaissance, comedy was seen as a form that had a clear moral purpose:

"The Poets devised to have many parts played at once by two, three or four persons, that debated the matters of the world, sometimes of their own private affairs, sometimes of their neighbours, but never meddling with any princes matters nor such high personages, but commonly of merchants, soldiers, artificers, good honest householders, and also of unthrifty youths, young damsels, old nurses, bawds, brokers, ruffians and parasites, with such like, in whose behaviours, lies in effect the whole course and trade of man's life, and therefore tended altogether to the good amendment of man by discipline and example. It was also much for the solace and recreation of the common people by reasons of the pageants and the shows. And this kind of poem was called Comedy."
(The Art of Poesie by George Puttenham, 1589)

All these elements are present in Shakespeare's comedies. The titles of the plays alone reveal that they are about groups of people rather than named individuals. The relationships between couples is the predominant plot device and the narrative movement towards joy – and the interest in sex – evident in the marriages that are the conclusion to all the comedies. Shakespeare, however, was not simply writing to a formula. His comedies contain distinctive features that have ensured their survival and popularity. His unique manipulation of place, shifting his characters (and therefore his audiences) from the known to the unknown, creates the memorable wood of *A Midsummer Night's Dream*, the Forest of Arden in *As You Like It*, Windsor Forest in *Merry Wives* and the forest, with outlaws, that is the setting for parts of *The Two Gentlemen of Verona*. Shakespeare populates these dramatically exciting locales with appealing characters – the clowns with their facility for wordplay and song and particularly those who in modern parlance might be considered the victims; the flawed, the confused and the vulnerable. Thus he presents misguided lovers, the fickle Proteus in *The Two Gentlemen of Verona* and the confused pairs in *A Midsummer Night's Dream*; the worthy Mechanicals, Bottom in *A Midsummer Night's Dream* and the well-meaning

Plautus Comicus

Shakespeare clearly knew many of the great classic authors – Plutarch, Ovid, Homer, Virgil and Seneca – some of whom were published in translation during his lifetime and others he may have studied in Latin at school. The work of the Roman comic dramatist Plautus was often studied in schools and it is his *Menaechmi* and *Amphitruo*, with his characteristic plots of mistaken identity, that are the source stories for Shakespeare's *Comedy of Errors*.

ABOVE Much Ado About Nothing *(here with Judi Dench as Beatrice and Donald Sinden as Benedick, RSC, 1976) affords many opportunities for disguise, overhearing and comic stage business.*

BELOW *Rosalind (Alexandra Gilbreath), disguised as Ganymede, in Arden forest with Touchstone (Adrian Schiller) and the shepherd Corin (Barry McCarthy) in* As You Like It *(RSC, 2000) with distinctive designs by Kaffe Fassett.*

BELOW RIGHT *The Mechanicals' play for the court in* A Midsummer Night's Dream *(here in the RSC 1999 production) requires precise comic timing and is one of the most popular moments on the Shakespearian stage.*

members of the Watch in *Much Ado About Nothing*; the orphans and lost siblings who occur throughout the genre; and, most memorably for many audiences, the witty and vulnerable women such as Beatrice, Sylvia and Rosalind.

In many comedies the vulnerability – and the humour and the romance – is reinforced through disguise as the young women dress as young men for protection and to allow them to travel. As the women's roles were acted by young men on the Shakespearian stage such a disguise must have been a multi-layered joke. While many have argued that such a plot device added to the erotic substance of the plays, this was surely not the case when Falstaff, in *Merry Wives*, disguises himself as "the fat woman of Brentford" to evade discovery by Master Ford, the jealous husband of one of the eponymous wives.

ABOVE LEFT *The lifelike ass's head used by David Troughton as Bottom ("This is to make an ass of me") in* A Midsummer Night's Dream *(RSC, 1989).*

ABOVE RIGHT *The fat Falstaff of* The Merry Wives of Windsor *(being duped and teased by Mistress Page and Mistress Ford) portrayed in this Robert Smirke painting, became a popular stereotype on and off stage.*

PANEL RIGHT *Over 130 plays are attributed to the Roman comic dramatist Plautus and his work was popular throughout the sixteenth century.*

The Comedies

DISTORTING THE CONVENTIONS

Shakespearian comedy begins darkly: news of the war opens *Much Ado*; *As You Like It* starts with Orlando's account of his mistreatment by his brother; Orsino is love-sick and Viola shipwrecked at the beginning of *Twelfth Night*. Some even start with death threats: the opening dialogue of *The Comedy of Errors* is between Egeon, a merchant from Syracuse who has landed, against the prevailing law, in Ephesus, and Solinus, the Duke of Ephesus, who will impose the death penalty for this transgression.

ABOVE *Peter O'Toole as Shylock in* The Merchant of Venice *(1960). The role has been played as a villain and a victim, and as a comic and tragic figure.*

RIGHT *The threatening, confusing world that Egeus (Richard Cordery, centre) encounters in Ephesus was partly conveyed by puppets in the RSC's 2005* Comedy of Errors.

BELOW *Londoners were interested in their commercial competitor Venice and Shakespeare used it as the setting for* Othello *as well as* The Merchant of Venice *(seen here in a set design for the play).*

In the opening scene of *A Midsummer Night's Dream*, Egeus insists that his daughter Hermia weds Demetrius or be put to death. Dark moments are sustained throughout the plots – many find the treatment of Malvolio, the aspiring steward in *Twelfth Night,* cruel rather than comedic – yet all these plays (and because of, not in spite of, their harsh openings) end neatly and romantically.

Not all Shakespeare's comedies offer such satisfying certainties, however. In some the ambiguities, particularly in the closing scenes, and the discomfort experienced by stage character and audience alike, have led to the label "problem play". It is as if Shakespeare is stretching or distorting the conventions of comedy. It is the setting, the structure and the characterization of the problem plays – *The Merchant of Venice, The Taming of the Shrew* and *Measure for Measure* – that sets them apart from others in the genre and contributes to their disturbing quality. The immediate difference is that they are set in a recognizable world rather than a supernatural, pastoral or classical milieu; they are firmly grounded in an Elizabethan/Jacobean reality. The multi-cultural and prejudiced world of *Merchant*, evident in the commercial activities of the city and in Portia's suitors, was not dissimilar to the world of the original London audiences. *Shrew*, in a scene that is sometimes cut in modern productions, opens with a drunken Christopher Sly

being thrown out of a Warwickshire alehouse and discovered by a lord with a hunting party. The hounds – Belman, Merriman, Clowder and Silver – reinforce the sense that this is an English play, before the travelling players arrive and the scene shifts to Italy. *Measure*, while ostensibly set in Vienna, contains a number of allusions to contemporary events (the plague, street brawling) that place the action, to all intents and purposes, in London in the early reign of King James.

It is the endings of the plays that makes them most uncomfortable. *Merchant* comes closest to the conventional

GIOVANNI BOCCACCIO
1313–75

Born in Florence, Boccaccio is best known as the author of the *Decameron* and influenced Chaucer as well as Shakespeare. His eye-witness account of the Black Death in 1348 opens the *Decameron*, a series of 100 tales ostensibly recounted over ten days by a group of young men and women taking refuge from the disease in a villa outside Florence. William Painter translated some of the tales into English in his *Palace of Pleasure* (1566–7) and Shakespeare drew on this work for the plot of *All's Well that Ends Well* and the wager plot of *Cymbeline*.

RIGHT *Viola disguised as the young man Cesario (Zoe Wanamaker) in Twelfth Night (RSC, 1983) is the catalyst for tangled relationships at Orsino's court and in Olivia's household.*

BELOW RIGHT *David Suchet's Shylock costume – the black gabardine the text requires – in a modern dress Merchant of Venice (RSC, 1981).*

BELOW *Vanessa Redgrave's costume in The Taming of the Shrew (RSC, 1961). Dressing Kate in bright colours is a common way of showing her assertive nature.*

BOTTOM LEFT *Michael Bogdanov's powerful staging of the final scene of The Taming of the Shrew as men wager for their wives' obedience. Kate (Paola Dionisotti, standing) shames her husband Petruccio (Jonathan Pryce, seated front right) with the bitterness of her compliance (RSC, 1978).*

PANEL RIGHT *The final moments of Measure for Measure: far removed from the happy marriages of romantic comedy, the couples are forced into reluctant unions.*

BELOW MIDDLE *In one of the many dark moments of The Merchant of Venice, Shylock comes close to removing his "pound of flesh" from Antonio.*

BELOW RIGHT *Malvolio (Philip Voss) is duped into believing that the Lady Olivia, his employer, has written him a love letter. Hidden in the hedge, the originators of the trick, Sir Toby Belch (David Calder), Sir Andrew Aguecheek (John Quayle) and Fabian (Malcom Scates), observe the success of their plot (Twelfth Night, RSC, 1997).*

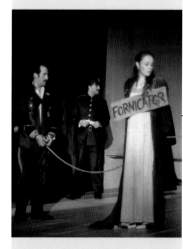

25

happy, coupling conclusion yet it is hard to take pleasure in the relationships between Portia and Bassanio, and Nerissa and Graziano after the humiliation of Shylock (and his exit) at the end of the fourth act. Katherine's "submission" speech at the end of *Shrew* presents similar difficulties:

"A woman moved is like a
   fountain troubled,
Muddy, ill-seeming, thick,
   bereft of beauty,
And while it is so, none so dry or thirsty
Will deign to sip or touch one drop of it.
Thy husband is thy lord, thy life,
   thy keeper…"
(Act 5, Scene 2)

John Fletcher's early seventeenth-century response to *Shrew*, *The Woman's Prize or the Tamer Tamed*, in which Petruccio is "tamed" by his new wife Maria following Kate's death, suggests that contemporary audiences found Shakespeare's play as uncomfortable (or as in need of challenging) as modern viewers.

Measure for Measure, however, is Shakespeare's most subversive comedy. There is no romance: the sexual relationships in the corrupt, hypocritical city state are bizarre (as in the "bedtrick" drawn from Boccaccio) or commercial and threatening. The "coupling" of the ending makes this explicit: Lucio, the clown, is to be married to a whore and then imprisoned; Angelo is to marry the woman he had previously jilted; Claudio is to marry the woman he made pregnant, and the Duke (who, disguised as a friar, has stage managed the plot until this point and now, in his own persona, arranges the conclusion) proposes to Isabella, the novice nun. It is Isabella's refusal to sleep with Angelo, in order to save her brother Claudio's life, that has been the moral dilemma at the heart of this disturbing play.

Such challenges have made this group of plays very popular on stage where they are frequently updated and performed in modern dress so that the problems they pose about race, religion and gender acquire a twenty-first-century relevance.

The "bedtrick", a plot device that Shakespeare used in *All's Well that Ends Well* and *Measure for Measure*, is derived from the ninth story of Boccaccio's *Decameron*. As a reward for curing the King of France, Gilette of Narbonne marries Bertrand of Roussillon against his will. He leaves her and establishes a relationship with another woman with whom he has two children. In fact, the women have changed places and he is sleeping with Gilette all along. As a comedic device the "bedtrick" may strain an audience's credulity, but it offers actors and directors the opportunity to comment on sexual relationships.

The History Plays:
THE FIRST TETRALOGY

Heminges and Condell list ten plays in the Histories section of the Catalogue (the contents list) of the First Folio. They are arranged not in the order they were written, but chronologically, using the dates of the monarchs who give the plays their titles – from *The Life and Death of King John*, who reigned from 1199 to 1216, to *The Life of King Henry the Eight* [sic].

ABOVE *William Hogarth's oil painting of David Garrick as Richard III, recording his famous "start" as he sees visions before the Battle of Bosworth, became a best-selling print.*

BELOW *Many subsequent actors have found it difficult to erase the distinctive sound of Laurence Olivier's delivery of "Now is the winter of our discontent..." in his influential film of Richard III.*

PANEL AND BACKGROUND *Holinshed's Chronicles are the major source for Macbeth, King Lear and Cymbeline as well as the English history plays.*

The first of these is amongst the least performed of Shakespeare's plays. Indeed there is no record of any staging of it at all until 1737 when the Shakespeare Ladies Club, a group of literary, patriotic philanthropists, promoted a production at Covent Garden. *Henry VIII* is very different from the others in the group as it is the closest that Shakespeare came to writing about contemporary events. It was written as late as 1613 in collaboration with John Fletcher, and concludes with the baptism of Elizabeth I and an allusion to King James. It is best considered not as a "history", but as a "late" play. Topped and tailed then, the Folio list of plays divides into two groups of four, often called tetralogies, that deal with consecutive events: the three parts of *Henry VI* and *Richard III* form the first tetralogy; *Richard II*, the two parts of *Henry IV* and *Henry V* the second.

The *Henry VI* plays are rarely performed and stand alone as single plays, but they have worked very well on stage when, cut or elided, they have been grouped with *Richard III* and presented as *The Wars of the Roses* (Peter Hall and John Barton for the Royal Shakespeare Company, 1963–4; Michael Bogdanov and Michael Pennington for the English Shakespeare Company, 1986) or *The Plantaganets* (Adrian Noble, RSC, 1988). The dramatic effectiveness of the death of the heroic Talbot and the English engagement with Joan la Pucelle (Joan of Arc) from Part One was evident in Michael Boyd's presentation of the Histories cycle for the RSC in 2000, performed in the small Swan theatre. The production of *King John* as part of the same project and in the same

space revealed humour as well as pathos in the work. A play whose popularity was confined to nineteenth-century productions that added spectacular off-text moments, such as the signing of Magna Carta, was reclaimed for the theatre.

Richard III, however, is much more frequently performed and has been popular with audiences from the moment it was written – it was published six times in quarto before the 1623 Folio. Its contemporary popularity is not difficult to understand. The story of Richard was well known through Shakespeare's source material and it is an immensely patriotic tale that affirms the introduction of the Tudor dynasty and, in Richmond's final speech, celebrates idealized Elizabethan values: piety, concern for the dead, a stress on mercy and justice and an appeal to the audience to preserve the hard won peace. Before this moment is reached, however, Shakespeare offers a tale of ambition, politics and power, explorations of good and evil, a serial killer (albeit by proxy), a strong dash of sex, superstition and the supernatural and, in addition to Richard himself, the hate figure of Queen Margaret, despised because she was French. A potential difficulty of dramatizing any familiar moment from history

TOP RIGHT *Shakespeare presents Joan of Arc (1412–31) with a strong anti-French bias in 1 Henry VI.*

RIGHT *Charles Kemble was a memorable King John at Covent Garden in the 1820s, wearing historically accurate costumes designed by Planché.*

SOURCES

English history plays were popular in the second half of the sixteenth century partly because of the nationalism that accompanied the break from the Roman Catholic church and also because of the availability of source material. For the *Henry VI* plays and *Richard III*, Shakespeare drew heavily on Edward Halle's *Union of the Two Noble and Illustrious Families of Lancaster and York* (1548) and Raphael Holinshed's *Chronicles of England, Scotland and Ireland* (1587). *Henry VIII* draws on Foxe's *Book of Martyrs* (1563) that celebrated Protestantism and was very popular during Elizabeth's reign.

ABOVE *Henry VI (Alan Howard in the RSC's 1978 production) is surrounded by powerful noblemen, having just been crowned by the Bishop of Winchester.*

BELOW *Guy Henry as King John (RSC, 2001) found humour and pathos in the role.*

is that the audience knows how the story will end and *Richard III* is a fine example of the way Shakespeare overcomes such difficulty. Firstly, he exploits the audience's knowledge: Richard's long opening speech announces that he is a villain and, through the use of soliloquy, makes the audience complicit in what follows. They are subsequently engaged through the speed of the action and Richard's brazen approach to murder and courtship. The pace is supported through Richard's humour and comic detachment and by some remarkably vivid imagery (he is described as a toad, a spider, a hedgehog, a dog, a hell-hound, a rooting hog) and the effect is to keep the audience listening as well as watching.

The further appeal is that from Colley Cibber's eighteenth-century production onwards the play has been a star vehicle. The range of the title role has attracted some great actors as it calls for sardonic humour, witty malevolence, savage ferocity, introspection, hysteria and finishes with a dramatic fight. It is also a challenge because of the physical demands of the role – the character is on stage almost the whole time, he is usually played with some obvious disability that can be tiring to sustain and he is so central to the action, driving the narrative, that there are few moments when the actor can coast. David Garrick, Sir Laurence Olivier (indelibly associated with Peter Sellers' "A Hard Day's Night" parody), Anthony Sher (performing on and with crutches) and Sir Ian McKellen (in a 1930s setting) have created memorable Richards and helped make this one of Shakespeare's best known history plays.

LEFT *Anthony Sher carefully researched disabilities and his acrobatic use of crutches made for a memorable, spider-like Richard III in the RSC's 1984 production.*

RIGHT *Henry VI (David Oyelowo in the RSC's 2000 production) despairs among the emblems of the warring Yorkists (white) and Lancastrians (red).*

Cibber adapted *Richard III* in 1699, making the title role, which he played himself, even more dominant than in the original so that he had about 40 per cent of the total dialogue and an additional seven soliloquies. He added chunks of *Henry V*, *Henry VI* and *Richard II*, but cut characters, including Margaret, Clarence, Edward IV and Hastings, reducing the cast list from 57 to 31. Many of these changes endured: despite minor attempts at restoration at Covent Garden in 1820, by Samuel Phelps in 1845 and by Henry Irving in 1877. Cibber's version was still being performed in 1909. Even in modern productions, Queen Margaret is cut (she is missing from the Olivier and McKellen films) and Cibber's dialogue survives: "Richard is himself again" and "Off with his head. So much for Buckingham" are Cibber not Shakespeare.

The History Plays
THE SECOND TETRALOGY

The four plays of the second tetralogy – Richard II, the two parts of *Henry IV* and *Henry V* – were written later than those of the first, although they deal with earlier events and offer a more sophisticated and ambiguous interrogation of kingship and politics. This is particularly obvious in *Richard II*, so politically sensitive that it was published and performed in Elizabeth's lifetime without the key "deposition" scene in which Richard abdicates in favour of Henry Bolingbroke, the future Henry IV.

ABOVE *The spectacular staging and use of crowds contributed to the success of Charles Kean's 1859 Henry V.*

RIGHT *The casting of Fiona Shaw as Richard II in Deborah Warner's 1995 production (RNT) was unusual, but shed light on the vulnerability and sometimes child-like petulance of the king.*

PANEL RIGHT *John Gielgud's superlative verse speaking revived interest in Richard II in the 1930s.*

The play remained controversial and, after the Restoration, Nahum Tate's 1680 adaptation was banned by the Crown.

Written entirely in verse (and with many of the beautiful passages, such as Gaunt's "This royal throne of kings, this sceptred isle" speech having a life beyond the stage) *Richard II* debates the nature of kingship and with a focus on language rather than action. The play did not become popular on stage until Charles Kean's nineteenth-century spectacular that added a procession, with crowds and real horses, for Bolingbrokes' entry into London. John Gielgud was responsible for the twentieth-century appreciation of the play: his beautiful verse-speaking was most appropriate for a drama that has the longest average speech length in the canon and his performances at the Old Vic in 1929–30 with Ralph Richardson as Bolingbroke and in 1937, with Michael Redgrave, became legendary.

But the play is amenable to many critical and staging approaches: recognizing that Richard and Bolingbroke change places physically, psychologically

and symbolically, the roles were alternated by Ian Richardson and Richard Pasco in the RSC production of 1973; and, in 1995, Deborah Warner explored Richard's ambiguous sexuality by casting Fiona Shaw in the title role of her production at the National Theatre.

While the two parts of *Henry IV* continue to explore kingship through Henry's anxieties and guilt and the un-king-like behaviour of his son (Prince Hal, the future Henry V), they are probably less memorable for their depiction of monarchy than for the characters of Shakespeare's subversive comic subplot: Falstaff and Mistress Quickly in Part One and, additionally, Doll Tearsheet and Justices Shallow and Silence in Part Two. Falstaff became a popular figure in the eighteenth century, the subject of comic sequels (such as *Falstaff's Wedding*), pictures and songs. He does not survive into *Henry V*, although Mistress Quickly gives a moving account of his death, and while the final play of the tetralogy retains some humour, including Princess Catherine learning English and her subsequent wooing by Henry in Act Five, it has a narrower focus: the defeat of the French. Some productions have sought to downplay the heroic elements of this patriotic myth but the power of Henry's rhetoric almost always defeats such attempts. While this war

JOHN GIELGUD
1904–2000

One of the greatest British actors and directors and the great nephew of Ellen Terry, Gielgud achieved Shakespearian distinction at the Old Vic in 1929, appearing as Antonio (*Merchant of Venice*) and Oberon as well as Richard II. His playing style was often contrasted with his more physical contemporary Olivier and was most apparent in the *Romeo and Juliet* of 1935 where they alternated the roles of Romeo and Mercutio. Best in serious, contemplative roles, he played Hamlet over 500 times. His distinctive voice is exploited in Peter Greenaway's 1991 film, *Prospero's Books*, where he spoke the whole text in addition to playing the lead.

Shakespeare had no direct experience of war, although for much of the period that he was writing plays England was under threat of invasion by the Spanish. His history plays explored civil war, rebellion and, most famously, war against France. What some see as Shakespeare's jingoism in *Henry V* is certainly off-set by the cynicism of Falstaff and his preference for life rather than honour (*1 Henry IV*) and his corrupt recruitment of soldiers from countrymen whose names alone – Ralph Mouldy, Simon Shadow, Thomas Wart, Francis Feeble, Peter Bullcalf – suggest their unsuitability for the task (*2 Henry IV*).

ABOVE Ian Richardson and Richard Pasco played the King and Bolingbroke as mirror images of each other in *Richard II* (RSC, 1973) and alternated roles.

LEFT Kenneth Branagh's historically detailed costume for *Henry V* (RSC, 1984), a role that he repeated in his film of 1989.

BELOW In a production that broke away from a period setting and gave the play contemporary relevance, William Houston as *Henry V* (RSC, 2000) rallies his troops before Agincourt.

has its savage elements – Bardolph's execution for looting and the killing of the French prisoners, for example – they are less memorable than the king's speech "Once more unto the breach, dear friends, once more" that concludes with "Cry 'God for Harry! England and Saint George!'", or his prayer on the eve of Agincourt, "O God of battles, steel my soldiers' hearts", or the moving St Crispin's day speech in which he addresses his troops as "We few, we happy few, we band of brothers".

Many have tried to discern Shakespeare's view of his historical past and political present through interpretation of his history plays. He is proposed as a monarchist, a cynic, a humanist, a believer in providence and the affairs of men. But, as with all efforts to read the author through his works, it is best to remember that he was a commercial man of the theatre: the plays are not personal manifestos, but dramas that work on stage.

ABOVE Here astride a cannon, Alan Howard was an inspirational Henry V in a performance influenced by Olivier's stirring film (RSC, 1975).

OPPOSITE Robert Stephens' performance as Falstaff in *1 Henry IV* in 1991 was a triumphant return to the Stratford stage and revealed unexpected depths in the role.

Tragedies
THE ILL-FATED HEROES

Eleven plays are listed in the "Tragedies" section of the Folio and three — *Coriolanus*, *Macbeth* and *Hamlet* — include the word "tragedy" in their titles. All 11, however, would have been recognized as tragedies according to the convention of the day because the titles are names, and nominate exceptional persons — kings, queens, rulers, and soldiers.

Conversely, there are no named persons in the titles of Shakespeare's comedies as, generically, they concern groups of people, have a broader focus, and are more concerned with the "ordinary" than the élite. In terms of their plots, of course, tragedies share more than a titular coincidence and are linked by the direction of their narratives — while they may begin joyfully, with a triumph in battle for example, they will conclude, inevitably, with death. Only the presence of *Cymbeline* in the Folio list subverts this convention, finishing with redemption and reconciliation rather than a body-strewn stage. The placement of this play, at the end of the volume, may be accounted for by the nature of its title (*Cymbeline King of Britain* identifies a named, important person) or pragmatic printing reasons.

It might be thought that with a focus on such persons and the nature of their violent deaths, surely beyond the experiences of most readers and audience members, the appeal of the tragedies would be lessened, but this is far from the case. Shakespeare's tragedies are his best-known works, worldwide, and the nature of the powerful emotions that they portray — love, jealousy, revenge, prejudice, patriotism — and the language in which they are expressed transcend specifics and give them a universal significance that has endured for 400 years. Different ages have re-created the tragic heroes in their own image: Hamlet for the Restoration and the eighteenth century was a frock-coated action man; for much of the nineteenth a thoughtful romantic, clad in black; while post-Freud he has become a psychologically troubled case for treatment, with a suspect relationship with his mother and his girlfriend. In communist, Eastern Europe he became a politicized figure, an embattled individual confronted with a totalitarian state.

Othello, too, has a diverse afterlife. Basing the plot on a short story by Cinthio, Shakespeare developed a character — the first black hero in English literature — who is isolated by race, military skill, an unauthorized marriage, and his credulous manipulation by the villain Iago. Despite murdering his innocent wife, Desdemona, his anguish and suffering are such that his appeal to audiences has endured. The full title of the play — *The Tragedie of Othello, the Moore of Venice* — gave the work a specific contemporary resonance. Shakespeare, like most Londoners, would have known of

GIOVANNI BATTISTA GIRALDI CINTHIO (1504–73)

Cinthio is the author of the collected stories *Hecatommithi*, which Shakespeare may have read in the original Italian and which provides the source tale for *Othello*. An ensign, named as Iago by Shakespeare, lusts after Disdemona and when she will not respond he plots her death, involving the Moor. Together, they club her to death with a sand-filled stocking then pull down the ceiling to disguise their action. Disdemona's family revenge her death by killing the Moor and torturing Iago, who dies horribly.

ABOVE *The African-American actor Ira Aldridge (1807–67) played Othello in London in 1825 and toured throughout Europe, dying in Lodz in Poland.*

ABOVE RIGHT *The lamp used by Henry Irving in Hamlet, an example of the historical detail that was typical of his productions in the late nineteenth century.*

BELOW *Patrick Stewart as a white Othello in a "photo-negative" production in Washington DC in 1998.*

PANEL *Paul Robeson first played Othello at the Old Vic in London in 1930 (here with Peggy Ashcroft as Desdemona) and was subsequently successful in the role on Broadway in 1943 and in Stratford in 1958.*

OPPOSITE *The Montagues and Capulets are distraught at the deaths of Romeo and Juliet (Ian McKellen and Francesca Annis in the RSC's 1976 production).*

OPPOSITE FAR RIGHT *Sam West, a powerful Hamlet in a modern-dress production by the RSC in 2001, considers "To be or not to be".*

ABOVE *Gertrude (Jane Lapotaire) tries to raise the spirits of her son Hamlet (Kenneth Branagh) in the RSC's 1992 production, which was given an Edwardian setting.*

BELOW *Original audiences may have associated Othello, the Moor of Venice, with Abdul Guahid, the Moorish Ambassador who visited Queen Elizabeth I in 1600.*

ARTHUR BROOKE
(d.1563)

the visit in 1600 to Queen Elizabeth of Abdul Guahid, the Moorish Ambassador, to discuss a joint project to take control of the East and West Indies from Spain. The Ambassador's portrait clearly shows an Arab with a white turban and highly decorated sword and scabbard, giving clues perhaps to Othello's original stage appearance. But Othello has been played on stage as a number of racial types and frequently by a white actor "blacked up". Indeed, some black actors, believing that Shakespeare endorses unattractive racial stereotypes, have refused to take the part. Throughout the nineteenth century, however, the play became known in Europe through the tours of the black American actor, Ira Aldridge, who contributed to the enduring popularity of the play in Russia. It was Stalin's favourite and he is thought to have responded to Othello's military prowess and his powerful speech – a reminder that context creates meaning.

Throughout *Hamlet* and *Othello* Shakespeare slowly builds the tension. While Hamlet, famously, delays taking revenge for his murdered father and Othello continues to be taken in by Iago's manipulations and insinuations, there are moments in both plays when the plots could turn: the outcome remains uncertain. *Romeo and Juliet* is a different sort of dramatic achievement because the audience, from the opening Prologue onwards (and due to knowledge of the tale from other sources, principally Arthur Brooke's poem), knows what is going to happen:

> "Two households, both alike in dignity
> In fair Verona, where we lay our scene,
> From ancient grudge break to new mutiny,
> Where civil blood makes civil hands
>   unclean.
> From forth the fatal loins of these two foes
> A pair of star-crossed lovers take their life…"

The pleasure in this play then may lie less in the plot than in the way the dramatist deals with it. In addition to giving a résumé of the story, the Prologue signals Shakespeare's concern with language: it is itself a sonnet, the audience will hear others and encounter examples of skilful, even ostentatious, wordplay – *Romeo and Juliet* is as much to do with words as swords.

The story of Romeo and Juliet was already well known throughout Europe when Shakespeare composed his play in around 1595. From an Italian story in Matteo Bandello's *Novelle*, which itself had precedents, it was translated into French in *Histoires tragiques* by Boaistuau and Belleforest, and then in 1562 the poet and translator Arthur Brooke created an English version, *The Tragical History of Romeus and Juliet*, a poem that is over 3,000 lines long. Shakespeare contracts the story, reducing Brooke's nine-month time span to less than a week and expanding minor characters, such as Tybalt, Mercutio and the Nurse.

Tragedies
THE FATE OF NATIONS

Both Romeo and Juliet and **Othello** are small scale, even domestic tragedies with plots that develop from doomed relationships. *King Lear* and *Macbeth*, however, have a broader focus and their plots concern the fate of nations – Scotland and England – as much as individuals. Both are Jacobean plays, probably written in 1606, and reflect a greater concern with good (or bad) governance and politics than the earlier plays.

ABOVE *John Singer Sargent's famous portrait of Ellen Terry as Lady Macbeth in 1888. Actual beetle wings were sewn on to her costume to give it a metallic sheen.*

BELOW *"Are ye fantastical or that indeed/which outwardly ye show?" Banquo challenges the three witches in Macbeth.*

While it is set in the past, the Porter's references to treason in *Macbeth* give it a contemporary political relevance, as it appears to allude to the conspirators of the Gunpowder plot.

These plays are, however, far removed from dry political discourse. While the stakes may be higher, both *Macbeth* and *Lear* feature compelling stage creations and have such an intense focus on heightened emotion that they make audiences acutely uncomfortable. Indeed, for many years, *Lear* was considered both un-actable and inappropriate to stage at all. The blinding of Gloucester, the death of Cordelia, the strange role of the Fool and the pessimistic hopelessness of the ending offended morally, religiously and aesthetically. There is a record of a single court performance on 26 December 1606, but from the Restoration until 1836 *King Lear* was staged only in Nahum Tate's adaptation. He cut the Fool, added a love plot between Cordelia and Edgar, and in preserving the lives of Gloucester, Kent and Lear turned what he described as a "Heap of Jewels, unstrung and unpolisht" into a more comfortable tale of "Regularity and Probability". In 1962, Peter Brook offered a powerful interpretation of the play that denied the audience any such comfort. The blinding of Gloucester took place immediately before the interval and the houselights came up as he was still crawling, bleeding and without help, from the stage.

The discomfort of *Macbeth* lies in the play's exploration of evil and ambition and, in some productions, the supernatural power of the witches. Such was the atmosphere created in Trevor Nunn's intimate presentation at the Other Place in

Stratford, with Ian McKellen and Judi Dench in 1976, that it was not unknown for audience members to hold up crosses to ward off evil.

Audiences and critics have also been unsettled by the presence, in both plays, of evil women and their complicity in violence, but attempts to soften or humanize their behaviour have rarely been successful. Ellen Terry tried for a more rounded presentation of Lady Macbeth in 1888 (a year when bloody deeds were much in the audience's mind as Jack the Ripper slashed his way through Whitechapel). She wanted to break from the "evil fiend" reading of the role established by Sarah Siddons, but the rather cosy result was

ABOVE *Ian McKellen and Judi Dench shocked audiences with their convincing depiction of evil in the RSC's small scale production of Macbeth, in 1976.*

RIGHT *The sword used by Paul Scofield during his performance of Macbeth in 1967. Apparently a copy of it was made and presented to local dignitaries while the company was on tour in Russia.*

THOMAS MIDDLETON
1580–1627

Middleton frequently collaborated with other dramatists, including Webster and Dekker, and it has always been difficult to be certain how much he worked with Shakespeare. Parts of *Timon* are probably his and scholars make a convincing case that he contributed to *Macbeth*: two of its songs first appeared in his play *The Witch*. The title pages of his *The Puritan* and *A Yorkshire Tragedy* give Shakespeare rather than Middleton as the author. His *Revenger's Tragedy* of 1606 has clear echoes of *Hamlet* and begins with the revenger, Vindice, holding and speaking to the skull of the woman he loved.

BELOW *A playbill for a nineteenth-century adaptation of* Timon of Athens *performed in Dublin with John Philip Kemble. Characteristically, the play was part of a mixed bill of entertainment.*

BOTTOM *The once generous, but now bankrupt, Timon of Athens (Michael Pennington) rails against "ingrateful man" as he digs in the earth (RSC, 1999).*

LEFT *The blinding of Gloucester in Peter Brook's production of* King Lear *(RSC, 1962) presented audiences with unremitting cruelty.*

BELOW *The power and wealth of the kingdom of King Lear (Eric Porter), displayed initially through ritual and the use of gold in costume and set, was eventually stripped away as the true nature of his children was revealed (RSC, 1968).*

PANEL RIGHT *Alec Guinness as the Fool in* King Lear *(1946–7).*

not well received. While the behaviour of Cordelia's wicked sisters, Goneril and Regan, may (in plot terms) be the result of Lear's unwise decision to divide his kingdom between his three daughters, the dynamics of the play are distorted if they become the sympathetic victims of bad parenting.

Timon of Athens was written at about the same time as *King Lear* and shares some of its sense of disillusionment, but is the least known and most rarely performed play in the canon. Until the nineteenth century it was only played in heavily adapted form and has rarely been seen on stage since. It is not difficult to account for its unpopularity: it seems unfinished, with less concern for character than for structure and the only roles for women are a group of Amazons, who perform in a masque, and two whores. There are also questions about its authorship. Thomas Middleton, possibly the author of an earlier Timon play performed at the Inns of Court, has been suggested as a co-dramatist and responsible for at least a third of the play. It has its supporters, though. Karl Marx, perhaps a surprising Shakespeare enthusiast, was impressed by Timon's tirade against the corrupting value of gold.

FOOLS

Both Lear and Timon include a character called simply "Fool" (a very small role in the latter). In Shakespeare's time, fools were servants at court or in large households and their function, dressed distinctively in cap and motley and carrying a curved stick, was to entertain. Some were professional fools, with a licence to speak that was denied other servants, but others were mental defectives whose odd behaviour was considered amusing. Feste in *Twelfth Night*, Lavatch in *All's Well that Ends Well* and Touchstone in *As You Like It* are jester-like, professional fools who entertain through wordplay and song.

Tragedies THE ROMAN PLAYS

In 1599, a Swiss traveller to London, Thomas Platter, described a visit to *Julius Caesar* and recorded that at the end "they danced together admirably and exceedingly gracefully, according to their custom, two in each group dressed in men's and two in women's apparel". A carefully choreographed jig may seem an unlikely end to one of the most serious plays in the canon.

ABOVE *In Yukio Ninagawa's Japanese* Titus Andronicus *(RSC, 2006) Lavinia's violated body is conveyed by red ribbons.*

RIGHT *Julius Caesar (Ian Hogg) is stabbed by the conspirators (RSC, 2001).*

Some of Shakespeare's tragedies are relieved by lighter or comedic moments (the Porter in *Macbeth*, the gravediggers in *Hamlet*) but the group of plays that Shakespeare based on Plutarch and usually called the Roman plays – *Titus Andronicus, Julius Caesar, Antony and Cleopatra* and *Coriolanus* – retain a serious tone and frequently a violent one.

Titus is Shakespeare's earliest tragedy and, some have argued, his first play – a judgement usually based on its perceived weaknesses. In 1687, Edward Ravenscoft described it as "the most incorrect and indigested piece in all his works; it seems rather a heap of Rubbish than a Structure", and T. S. Eliot went further in 1927, calling it "one of the stupidest and most uninspired plays ever written, a play in which it is incredible that Shakespeare had any hand at all". The problem with its reception, as with *Lear*, lies with the violence of the plot, some of which is seen on stage and some is reported: Titus is tricked into cutting off his own hand, his sons are murdered, and his daughter is raped and has her tongue cut out so she cannot reveal the perpetrators. Titus takes revenge on the two rapists by killing them, baking them in a pie and serving them to their mother. Theatres usually have first-aiders on standby to deal with those who faint.

While the plot may repel, a sketch of the play by Henry Peacham has proved enduringly fascinating. Peacham graduated from Cambridge University in 1595 and the drawing is tentatively dated from that year. It clearly shows characters from

Shakespeare's play (and includes portions of text): Tamora, the Queen of the Goths with her two sons; Titus; Aaron, the black villain of the play, and a number of soldiers. It is not known if the scene comes from Peacham's imagination or is a record of what he saw on stage. If it is the latter, then it is the only contemporary illustration of a performance and its mixture of Roman and Elizabethan dress is a valuable record of theatre costume.

Titus, because of its subject matter, and *Antony and Cleopatra*, because of its familiarity and the specificity of its setting, have proved resistant to updating and modern dress. Indeed, one of the problems of staging *Antony and Cleopatra* has always been the desire to replicate Rome, Egypt, sea battles and the well-known appearance of Cleopatra. Even productions which try to simplify the staging or present original playing conditions have struggled to present Antony's death and to interpret the stage direction that instructs the Guard to "heave Antony aloft to Cleopatra". So, where and how could this have taken place on the bare Elizabethan stage? It may suggest the use of the balcony and the need for hoists, but the effect is potentially clumsy rather than tragic.

Julius Caesar and *Coriolanus*, however, have a rich theatrical afterlife, as the politics they explore clearly have relevance not only for the Roman age and Shakespeare's times, but also for subsequent ages. In 1937, Orson Welles presented

THOMAS PLATTER
1574–1682

Platter's account of *Julius Caesar*, written in German, is the first known description of a performance at the Globe, "the straw thatched house" as he called it. Born in Basle, he studied medicine at the University of Montpellier and then visited England in September and October 1599. The conclusion of a play with a jig seems to have been regular practice in the theatre with the comic actor Richard Tarlton the best known exponent. In 1999, the new Globe staged a 500th anniversary production of *Julius Caesar* and concluded the play with a jig as described by Platter.

PANEL ABOVE *An engraving of the actor Richard Tarlton.*

OPPOSITE *Orson Welles as Brutus in his modern dress, anti-fascist production of* Julius Caesar *(New York, 1937).*

Julius Caesar in the USA, subtitled "Death of a Dictator", as a comment on contemporary politics. Many productions since have chosen the 1930s, because of the rise of fascism, as an appropriate setting. The RSC production of 2001, for example, was set in 1930s Germany. In 1993, the same company had set the play in post-Cold War Eastern Europe and the assassination of Caesar was read by many reviewers of that production as a mirror of the fall of Ceausescu, the Communist dictator of Romania. Like Caesar, Coriolanus has been presented as a recognizable dictator of the 1930s, or as an aristocrat in the French Revolution (Paul Scofield in 1961 in Stratford, Ontario, or Toby Stephens in Stratford in the UK), or as a Japanese warrior (Stratford, UK), but the role is larger and more complex than Caesar and the mob that he antagonizes unattractive and fickle. The political debates of both plays are sophisticated and explore character as much as creed and their appropriation by right and left is in itself a fine example of Shakespeare "not of an age but for all time".

ABOVE LEFT *Setting the play in the French Revolution gave a new political meaning to the crowd scenes in David Thacker's production of* Coriolanus *(RSC, 1994).*

ABOVE RIGHT AND LEFT *The "infinite variety" of Cleopatra: Janet Suzman, above, berates a messenger (RSC, 1972); Helen Mirren, left, declares her love for Antony (Michael Gambon) (RSC, 1982).*

BELOW *Henry Peacham's sketch of* Titus Andronicus, *made c.1595, is the first known illustration of a Shakespeare play. Tamora pleads with Titus for the life of her sons.*

The best known work of the Greek essayist and philosopher Plutarch was *Parallel Lives* in which he also turned biographer and compared pairs of famous Greeks and Romans. Shakespeare knew the *Lives* in Sir Thomas North's English version of 1579, itself a translation from the French of Jacques Amyot, and used it extensively as a source for *Julius Caesar, Antony and Cleopatra* and *Coriolanus* and to a lesser extent *Titus. Antony and Cleopatra* also uses Plutarch's *Moralia*, translated in 1603 by Philemon Holland.

Late Plays and Collaborations

At the end of his career Shakespeare wrote a number of plays, some in collaboration with other dramatists, that are so different from the rest of the canon that they are frequently given a new generic label – not Comedy, History or Tragedy, although they contain elements of all three, but "late" or "last" plays and sometimes "romance". They include:

BELOW *Prospero (Alec McGowen) looks on as his daughter Miranda (Sarah Woodward) chides the "savage and deformed slave" Caliban (David Troughton) in* The Tempest *(RSC, 1993).*

Pericles (probably a collaboration with George Wilkins), written in 1608, but not published in the Folio.
The Winter's Tale, written in 1609–10, and in the Comedy section of the Folio.
Cymbeline, written in 1610–11, and in the Tragedy section of the Folio.
The Tempest, written in 1611, the first play in the Folio (in the Comedy section).
Henry VIII (probably a collaboration with John Fletcher), written in 1613, and in the History section of the Folio.
The Two Noble Kinsmen (a further collaboration with John Fletcher or possibly Philip Massinger), written in 1613–14, but not in the Folio.

Leaving aside *Kinsmen*, which is largely a dramatization of The Knight's Tale from Chaucer's *Canterbury Tales*, these late plays share more than a coincidence of date and have some intriguing common features that reinforce the inclination to group them together. The plots all concern powerful fathers and daughters (Pericles/Marina; Leontes/Perdita; Cymbeline/Imogen; Prospero/Miranda; Henry VIII/Mary and Elizabeth).

In each case the flawed father is clearly contrasted with the innocence of his daughter and, indeed, the women all suffer because of the men's intemperate behaviour. When Imogen disguises herself as a youth in *Cymbeline*, for example, it is not the comedic device of the earlier plays, but a necessity to save her life.

Implicit in each plot is a concern with power, rule, authority and succession: Prospero has been usurped; Henry VIII needs an heir; Leontes' son dies and his daughter is lost. Each play therefore has tragic potential and interrogates real pain and suffering, but instead of concluding with death the narrative flow changes direction and the plays end with regeneration and restoration: lost sons are found (*Cymbeline*); wives thought dead are returned to life (*Winter's Tale*); daughters' lives are celebrated (*Henry VIII*); dukedoms are restored (*Tempest*). These then are not realistic plots – some, such as *Cymbeline*, are closer to fairytales – and this sense of fantasy is reinforced by some of Shakespeare's most imaginative characterization (Ariel, Caliban, Cloten) and audacious stagecraft. *The Winter's Tale* statue that comes to life and its most famous stage

ABOVE *Paulina (Peggy Ashcroft) carefully stage-manages the ending of* The Winter's Tale *as the "statue" of Hermione (Elizabeth Sellars) comes to life, astounding her husband Leontes (Eric Porter) (RSC, 1960).*

ABOVE *The fairy-tale ending of Cymbeline as the King (Sebastian Shaw) is reunited with his daughter Imogen (Susan Fleetwood, seated left, in disguise) and his lost sons, Arviragus and Guiderius.*

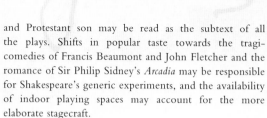

John Fletcher (1579–1625), who is best known for the tragi-comedies he co-authored with Francis Beaumont, succeeded Shakespeare as the principal dramatist of the King's Men. In addition to the published Shakespeare collaborations they are thought to have worked together on *Cardenio*, probably based on *Don Quixote*, that is now lost.

George Wilkins, of whom little is known, wrote the prose work *The Painful Adventures of Pericles, Prince of Tyre* in 1608. It is clearly a source for Shakespeare's *Pericles* and some scholars argue that they wrote the play together. Equally clear, however, is that it draws on the *Confessio Amantis* of Chaucer's contemporary John Gower who is incorporated into the play as its Chorus and storyteller.

Philip Massinger (1583–1640) wrote for the King's Men sometimes in collaboration with Fletcher and succeeded him as their major dramatist. Some propose Massinger rather than Fletcher as the co-author of *Henry VIII* and *The Two Noble Kinsmen*.

direction – "Exit, pursued by a bear" – or the magic that permeates *The Tempest* or the headless body in *Cymbeline* are all examples of a confident playwright at the height of his powers. And these bravura moments are matched by some of the most beautiful verse passages in the canon.

Some commentators have tried to account for the late plays' differences through speculative biography, suggesting that Shakespeare must have doted on his daughters or perhaps wished to put right a difficult relationship. Others see something religious in the redemptive element of the plots and posit a development in Shakespeare's spiritual life. Lytton Strachey argued that the playwright was simply bored with conventional theatre. It should be remembered, however, that Shakespeare was a practical dramatist and an astute businessman and the differences are more explicable (and more quantifiable) in contextual rather than biographical terms. New World discoveries and the wreck in Bermuda inform character and plot in *The Tempest*. Political and religious insecurities exacerbated by the Gunpowder Plot and concerns about the succession following the premature death of Prince Henry, King James' eldest, popular and Protestant son may be read as the subtext of all the plays. Shifts in popular taste towards the tragi-comedies of Francis Beaumont and John Fletcher and the romance of Sir Philip Sidney's *Arcadia* may be responsible for Shakespeare's generic experiments, and the availability of indoor playing spaces may account for the more elaborate stagecraft.

Whatever the cause of the new styles evident in his last works, Shakespeare's career ended on a high note. The most enduring biographical reading of the plays is that in *The Tempest*. Shakespeare, through Prospero, is saying farewell to the stage. While clearly, from the evidence of the collaborative works, this is not true, the sentiment is very appealing and may have been tacitly acknowledged by Hemminges and Condell when they positioned the play as the first in the Folio.

LEFT *Henry VIII (Donald Sinden) rejoices at the birth of his daughter, the future Queen Elizabeth, while her mother, Anne Bullen (Lisa Harrow) looks on (RSC, 1970).*

RIGHT *King James' popular and eldest son and theatre patron, Prince Henry, who died young in 1612.*

BACKGROUND *The signed testimony of Guy Fawkes in which he confesses his involvement in the Gunpowder Plot to assassinate King James I in 1605.*

Shakespeare's Poems

Some controversy surrounds Shakespeare's poetry. Exactly what did he write and to whom, in the case of the sonnets, was he writing? Poems were published during his lifetime and have been attributed to him since whose provenance is far from certain. In 1599, for example, William Jaggard published *The Passionate Pilgrim*. By W. Shakespeare which contains, in addition to two Shakespearian sonnets and poems from *Love's Labour's Lost*, verses that are clearly written by others, including Marlowe and Raleigh.

More recently the Oxford Collected Works (1988) has included the nine-stanza love poem "Shall I die", and from 1989 strong claims have been made for "A Funeral Elegy". There are strong doubts about the authorship of both these works.

Undoubtedly, however, Shakespeare wrote the two long narrative poems, *Venus and Adonis* and *The Rape of Lucrece*, probably between 1592 and 1594 when the London theatres were closed due to the plague. Based on Ovid, they are both very active, dramatic tales that employ dialogue (a feature that was exploited by Gregory Doran when he staged *Venus and Adonis* for the Royal Shakespeare Company using puppets in 2005). One is an erotic and funny tale – eventually rather moving – in which Venus pursues the unwilling Adonis, and the other a tragic tale of rape and suicide.

Controversy, enigmas and questions surround Shakespeare's sonnets. First published in 1609, but probably written from the 1590s onwards, the dedication at the front of the book raises the first uncertainties:

TO.THE.ONLY.BEGETTER.OF.
THESE.ENSUING.SONNETS.
MR.W.H.ALL.HAPPINESS.
AND.THAT.ETERNITY.
PROMISED.
BY.
OUR.EVER-LIVING.POET.
WISHETH.
THE.WELL-WISHING.
ADVENTURER.IN.
SETTING.
FORTH.
T.T.

ABOVE *Hilliard's miniature has been tentatively identified as a number of young men of the period, including Robert Devereux, the Earl of Essex, and Shakespeare himself. Garrick used the pose as the model for the statue of Shakespeare that he commissioned for his temple.*

BELOW *"When in the world I lived I was the world's commander": Nathaniel the Curate impersonates Alexander the Great to entertain the young lovers in the final scene of* Love's Labour's Lost, *one of the plays in which Shakespeare refers directly to Ovid (RSC, 1985).*

OVID

43BC–AD17

Ovid was the favourite, most read and most influential classical author of the period. Shakespeare would have studied him at school in the original Latin and read Arthur Golding's English translation of 1567. He refers to Ovid directly in *As You Like It* and *Love's Labour's Lost*. The bulk of Shakespeare's classical allusions are drawn from Ovid's major work, the *Metamorphoses*, which also provides the source story for *Venus and Adonis*. The principle source for *The Rape of Lucrece* is Ovid's *Fasti*.

The Italian poet and humanist's love poems to Laura (identity unknown) established the style and subject matter not only of Shakespeare's sonnets, but also the work of many Elizabethan writers, most notably Sir Philip Sidney's sonnet sequence *Astrophil and Stella* of 1591, and Edmund Spenser's *Amoretti* of 1595. Mercutio teases Romeo with references to Petrarch and Laura in *Romeo and Juliet*, a work that includes sonnets, in Act 2, Scene 3.

RIGHT *Titian's "Rape of Lucretia". Raped at knifepoint by Tarquin, son of the Roman king, Lucretia subsequently stabbed herself to death.*

BELOW LEFT *A scene from Gregory Doran's innovative staging of Venus and Adonis that used puppets to illustrate the drama of the poem (RSC, 2005).*

BELOW MIDDLE *Penelope, Lady Rich has been suggested as the "Dark Lady" to whom some of the sonnets are addressed.*

BELOW RIGHT *The Earl of Southampton, Shakespeare's patron, perhaps the "Fair Youth" of the Sonnets .*

"T.T." may be assumed to be the publisher, Thomas Thorpe, but "MR.W.H." remains unidentified. Some suggest Shakespeare's patron, Henry Wriothesley, the Earl of Southampton (HW reversed to WH); some Southampton's stepfather Sir William Harvey; others William Herbert, the Earl of Pembroke. It is not clear if Mr. W. H. is the "begetter", meaning perhaps a patron, or possibly the inspirer, or even the author. The next question concerns the "voice" of the sonnets. Clearly they are written in the first person – "Shall *I* compare thee to a summer's day?" (Sonnet 18), or "No longer mourn for *me* when *I* am dead" (Sonnet 71) – but this voice may not reflect personal feeling. The sonnets may be as imaginative or as fictional as the plays or they may be exercises in sonnet form or even commissioned works. Frequently, however, they are read as

an autobiography, generating further conjecture as the first 126 sonnets are clearly written to or about a man (the "Fair Youth") and all but the final two of the remainder (127–152) to a woman (the "Dark Lady"). This raises questions about Shakespeare's sexual orientation, an anxiety that is evident perhaps in the second publication of the sonnets, in 1640 by John Benson, when the sequences of the verses were changed and some of the language altered so that fewer were addressed to a man. Those who read them as an account of Shakespeare's emotional life and have searched for the identity of the unnamed male and female subjects have produced candidates as unlikely as any of the authorship contenders. Penelope, Lady Rich, Mary Fitton and Emilia Lanier may be the most credible claimants for the "Dark Lady", but Elizabeth I, Jane, the wife of theatre impresario Sir William Davenant, and Cleopatra are simply fanciful. The major candidates for the "Fair Youth" – the Earl of Southampton (again), William Herbert (again) and Robert Devereux, the Earl of Essex, have at least a documented connection with Shakespeare.

Such speculation inevitably diverts attention from the sonnets themselves. Less well known than the plays, they are nevertheless amongst Shakespeare's greatest achievements. Developing from their Petrarchan progenitors, they demonstrate a skill with language and a control of form, a manipulation of idea and strong emotion, and a remarkable amalgamation of style and content that has never been surpassed.

The Jacobean Stage

In 1603, on the death of Elizabeth I, King James (already the King of Scotland, where he was known as a writer and patron of drama) ascended the throne and became patron of Shakespeare's theatre company, which was renamed the King's Men.

This important connection and change of status is acknowledged in at least three plays: *Macbeth*, which includes a sanitized representation of James' ancestor Banquo as well as reflecting his interest in witchcraft; *Measure for Measure* where the interest in governance and, particularly, the figure of the disguised Duke mirror the King's interests; and *Othello*, whose partial setting in Cyprus and the war with the Turks are the subjects of a long poem, "Lepanto" written by James.

For the first five years of James' reign the King's Men continued to perform at the Globe, but in 1608 the company acquired Blackfriars, an indoor playing space that was a former monastery and had recently been used by boy actors, on the north bank of the Thames. It was not employed immediately because of an outbreak of plague, but from 1609 it became their winter home. Its difference from the open-air Globe had a clear influence on the plays and the way they were performed. The stage was situated

across the narrow side of a rectangular hall and the audience, all seated, viewed the show from the front or from galleries around three sides. Performances were candle-lit and the need to trim wicks or replace the candles was responsible for the development of intervals: plays were now divided into five acts with music performed between them. However simple, lighting – or the lack of it – could create special effects or moods impossible to achieve in daylight. With a stronger structure and a roof, machinery could be employed to allow for the descent of gods and supernatural creatures. When the Globe was rebuilt after the fire of 1613, it too had such potential and, while it is thought that *The Winter's Tale* and *Cymbeline* were written specially for performances at Blackfriars, it was certainly possible to present them, and all the late plays, in both houses. Undoubtedly there was more to see on the Jacobean stage as the visual experience began to match the auditory one.

ABOVE *Macbeth, here with Roger Allam in the title role and Philip Quast as Banquo (RSC, 1996), reflected King James' interests and acknowledged his ancestor, Banquo.*

RIGHT *Part of Visscher's panorama of London showing St Paul's Cathedral on the north bank of the Thames and the Globe on the south.*

PANEL RIGHT *Inigo Jones whose designs revolutionized court entertainments.*

BACKGROUND *The palace of Whitehall, where Shakespeare and his fellow actors would have performed.*

INIGO JONES
1573–1652

Best known as an architect who became Surveyor of the Office of Works in 1615, Jones was responsible for the classical designs of Whitehall Banqueting House in the centre of London and the Queen's House in Greenwich. His travels in Italy and elsewhere on the Continent influenced not only his architecture, but also the remarkable structures and costume designs that he created for court entertainments: replicas of double-tiered, classical buildings where the upper storey revolved or whose doors opened to allow access for chariots, transformation scenes and detailed head-dresses for classical queens.

LEFT *Inigo Jones' design for a lord performing as a star in the Lords' Masque of 1613 written by Thomas Campion.*

BELOW *Cymbeline (here in the moment when the British king refuses to pay the annual tribute to the Roman Augustus Caesar, SMT, 1957) may have been written specifically for performance at Blackfriars, the former monastery on the north bank of the Thames that Shakespeare's company purchased in 1608.*

Throughout this period the King's Men were performing Shakespeare's plays regularly at court, an experience that may also be reflected in the style of Shakespeare's later works. The dominant form of court entertainment was the masque, a form of show that had been used to celebrate special royal occasions for many years, but which reached new heights of extravagance and sophistication during James' reign. They were scripted works, frequently allegories, but the visual experience was paramount and achieved through design, dancing, acrobats, lighting, paint, music and mechanical skill.

The greatest exponents of the genre were the dramatist Ben Jonson and the architect Inigo Jones. For their first collaboration, on the *Masque of Blackness* in 1605, Jones created an artificial sea with a wave machine, a huge shell which rose from the waves to reveal the performers and a final revelation of a moon goddess who appeared suspended above the stage in a silver throne. Some of the participants were professional, and may have included members of the King's Men, but most were senior courtiers, women as well as men, entertaining each other on special occasions, such as Twelfth Night or Accession Day, or performing for visiting dignitaries and diplomats.

While few of these special effects could be achieved on the public stage – whether indoors or out – not least because of the expense, it is noticeable how many of Shakespeare's last plays call for visual displays, music and dance, and two, *The Tempest* and *Henry VIII* include masques.

The son of Mary Queen of Scots and Lord Darnley, James inherited his theatrical interests from his mother. Mary's first husband was François II of France and it was in France that she acquired a lifelong love of theatre that lasted up to, and included, her carefully choreographed execution, by Queen Elizabeth, in 1587. James' immediate family exhibited an equal (if less morbid) interest. His son, Prince Henry, and his wife, Queen Anne, were, like him, patrons of theatre companies and the royal court became the centre of cultural as well as political life: at least 14 of Shakespeare's plays were performed there.

Shakespeare's Return to Stratford

BELOW *The garden of New Place, the site of Shakespeare's home. The building was demolished in 1759 by Rev. Francis Gastrell, who was irritated by tourists asking to see where Shakespeare had lived.*

It is not certain how Shakespeare divided his time between London and Stratford, but it is clear that by 1598 his career as a dramatist was secure. Francis Meres, in *Palladis Tamia*, praised his skill and mentioned 12 of his plays as well as his "sugared Sonnets". He was evidently prosperous and a property owner. In 1597, he had purchased one of Stratford's largest houses, New Place, built by Hugh Clopton, and subsequently bought 107 acres of Stratford land and a cottage in Chapel Lane.

In 1605, records show that Shakespeare purchased an interest in a lease of the Stratford tithes which generated £60 a year. On his father's death in 1601 he had inherited the property in Henley Street (now known as the Birthplace) where he had gown up. Part of it was occupied by his sister Joan and the rest was let and became an inn.

In 1596, his father had been granted a coat of arms, almost certainly with Shakespeare's help at the College of Arms in London, and the distinctive shield with a spear (a pun on the family name), a falcon above it and the motto "Non Sans Droit" (not without right) was a further part of his inheritance plus the status of "gentleman" that went with it. The record of Shakespeare's death in the burial register appends "gent" by the side of his name.

There is some evidence of Shakespeare's involvement in local affairs – subscribing to the cost for prosecuting a bill in parliament in 1611 to repair the highways and some documentation of 1614, where his involvement in disputes concerning enclosures is difficult to interpret. Nothing, however, is known of his reaction to the serious Stratford fire of 1604 or the bad harvests of 1607–8 that caused significant poverty. He may well have been in Stratford for family affairs, such as his mother's burial in September 1608 and his daughters' marriages to John Hall and Thomas Quiney. But records place him in London in 1612 to give evidence in a legal case, known as the Belott-Mountjoy suit, and in 1613 when he purchased the Blackfriars Gatehouse.

JOHN HALL
c.1575–1635

A physician, educated at Queen's College, Cambridge, Hall married Shakespeare's daughter Susanna on 5 June 1607. Their daughter Elizabeth was born in February 1608. They lived first in the house now called Hall's Croft, then moved into New Place on Shakespeare's death. The house was demolished by Rev. Francis Gastrell in 1759 and he also cut down the mulberry tree, supposedly planted by Shakespeare. In 1613, Susanna sued John Lane for alleging that she had a venereal disease contracted from Ralph Smith. Lane failed to appear at the court in Worcester Cathedral and was excommunicated.

ABOVE *This sketch by George Vertue, drawn partly from memory in 1737, shows Shakespeare's home before it was destroyed.*

THOMAS QUINEY
1589–1662

A vintner who married Shakespeare's daughter Judith on 10 February 1616. Quiney helped run his widowed mother's business (when her husband died she had nine children under 20) and, by 1608, he was selling wine to Stratford Corporation. From 1611, he ran a tavern in the High Street. He was temporarily excommunicated from the church for marrying Judith during Lent and was in further trouble on 26 March 1616 when he was charged by the church court with making Margaret Wheeler pregnant. She, with her child, had been buried 11 days earlier. The careful terms of his will suggest that Shakespeare did not trust Quiney and he made some revisions after the Wheeler affair.

On 25 March 1616 Shakespeare signed his will and he died soon after on 23 April in Stratford. He was buried in Holy Trinity Church two days later.

John Ward, who was vicar of Stratford from 1662 until his death in 1681, collected anecdotes about Shakespeare and recorded the story that "Shakespeare, Drayton and Ben Jonson had a merry meeting and, it seems, drank too hard, for Shakespeare died of a fever there contracted", but there is no formal evidence of the cause of his death.

In his will, Shakespeare left substantial and clearly detailed bequests to family and friends, including colleagues from the King's Men, and while the document appears to be a straightforward distribution of effects it has always generated conjecture: are the three signatures in Shakespeare's hand; what happened to his books and manuscripts which are not mentioned; why is his wife left the "second best bed with the furniture"?

The memorial effigy in Holy Trinity Church, probably commissioned by Shakespeare's son-in-law John Hall and in place by 1622, was crafted by Geerhart Janssen and is likely to be the most accurate representation of the dramatist. It has become a site of pilgrimage for many Shakespeare enthusiasts but, perhaps because of the corpulent, provincial figure it portrays, has never been as well known as the Droeshout engraving from the Folio or as popular as the Chandos portrait which has been the model for many copies. So called because for some years it was in the possession of the Dukes of Chandos, its provenance is shaky. It is of the right period (although doubt has often been expressed that the earring is a later addition), attributed to John Taylor, and is thought to have belonged to William Davenant who, according to John Aubrey, claimed to be Shakespeare's illegitimate son. The three representations – Janssen, Droeshout and Chandos – may have less to do with verisimilitude, however, and much more to do with image. In each case the message conveyed is of intelligence (the large domed forehead housing a large brain), wealth (the elaborate collar or ruff) and class (the neatly trimmed facial hair).

GOOD FREND FOR IESVS SAKE, FORBEARE,
TO DIGG THE DVST ENCLOASED HEARE:
BLESE BE Y MAN Y SPARES THES STONES,
AND CVRST BE HE Y MOVES MY BONES.

Shakespeare During the Restoration

After the restoration of the monarchy in 1660, King Charles II granted royal patents to two theatre companies. Little had been written or staged during the 20-year theatre closure enforced by Oliver Cromwell's Puritan administration, so each of the new company's repertoires was largely made up of old plays, including Shakespeare. The King's Company, led by Thomas Killigrew, acquired those plays that had been performed by the old King's Men before 1642, and the Duke's Company, led by Sir William Davenant, obtained exclusive rights to some of the remainder, including *King Lear* and *The Tempest*.

ABOVE *William Davenant (1606–68), the playwright and theatre manager who headed the Duke's Company and adapted Shakespeare's plays.*

Davenant, who claimed to be Shakespeare's illegitimate son, was the more innovative of the two, introducing a flying machine, for example, and employing Thomas Betterton, the greatest actor of the period.

The old outdoor playing spaces, like the Globe, had not survived and the earliest Restoration performance spaces were adapted from real tennis courts and featured a deep thrust stage (around which the audience was seated on three sides in the pit, as well as in galleries or boxes) with side entrances in close proximity to the spectators. Even with such simple staging it was the visual experience that was emphasized, such as the singing and dancing that were popular additions to Davenant's *Macbeth* (1664) or the 1674 operatic version of *The Tempest*.

Both companies made significant changes to their Shakespeare texts to accommodate shifts in taste and the new playing conditions. John Dryden created a symmetrical adaptation of *The Tempest* adding "the Counterpart to Shakespeare's Plot, namely that of a Man who had never seen a Woman, that by this means those two characters of Innocence and Love might the more illustrate and commend each other". He also wrote a special prologue praising Shakespeare, but justifying the need for amendment and appealing for the audience's support:

> "As when a Tree's cut down the secret root
> Lives underground, and thence new Branches shoot;
> So, from old Shakespeare's honour'd dust, this day
> Springs up and buds a new reviving Play…
> But, if for Shakespeare we your grace implore,
> We for our Theatre shall want it more."

This became standard practice: the male lead, sometimes in role and sometimes as the ghost of Shakespeare, delivered a prologue and the performance concluded with an epilogue from the female lead.

During his exile abroad, King Charles had seen women on stage. The most significant development of this period was the introduction of actresses to the London theatres, marking the end of the transvestite tradition other than in comic roles,

PANEL ABOVE RIGHT *John Dryden, the greatest literary figure of the Restoration period, who adapted and promoted Shakespeare.*

LEFT *Theatres re-opened at the Restoration of Charles II in 1660, depicted here in a silk embroidery of 1665.*

JOHN DRYDEN
1631–1700

A distinguished poet, dramatist and prose writer, Dryden was created Poet Laureate by Charles II. In addition to adapting *The Tempest* with Davenant and *Troilus and Cressida* (1679), his *All for Love* (1678) was based on Shakespeare's *Antony and Cleopatra*. In his important critical work of 1688, *Essay of Dramatick Poesy*, he was among the first to identify Shakespeare as the genius of English drama and he subsequently defended Shakespeare against the attacks of Thomas Rymer (1641–1713) who ridiculed *Othello* as a "bloody Farce" and suggested it should be re-titled "The Tragedy of the Handkerchief".

Tate, a playwright and poet, was created Poet Laureate in 1692. His many talents included writing the libretto for Purcell's *Dido and Aeneas* and the words of "While Shepherds watched their Flocks by Night". He adapted *Richard II*, *Coriolanus* and, most notoriously, *King Lear* to which he gave a happy ending – Cordelia survives and marries Edgar. While it is easy now to scoff at such changes, Tate's popular version became the standard *Lear* and was performed regularly from 1681 until 1845.

such as the witches in Davenant's version of *Macbeth* and the Nurse in *Romeo and Juliet*. One outcome of this innovation was the addition of scenes of sex, violence and voyeurism. Some adaptations, such as Thomas Durfey's version of *Cymbeline,* included explicit threats of rape, and others, such as Colley Cibber's re-working of *Richard III*, included overwrought emotional speeches. Elizabeth Barry (c.1658–1713) is usually credited as the first English actress, working with Davenant and performing, mainly in tragedy, opposite Betterton. From 1695 Anne Bracegirdle (c.1663–1748) jointly managed Lincoln's Inn Fields with Betterton and Barry and her acting roles included Desdemona, Ophelia and, like Barry, a very affecting Cordelia in Nahum Tate's adaptation of *Lear*.

Such adaptations were once dismissed as risible, but without them it is doubtful whether Shakespeare would have survived on stage or achieved his status as the national poet.

ABOVE LEFT *Thomas Durfey (1653–1723), whose popular adaptation of* Cymbeline *added a new rape sub-plot.*

ABOVE MIDDLE *The actor, manager and dramatist Thomas Killigrew (1612–81) headed the King's Company at the Restoration.*

ABOVE RIGHT *The roles of Elizabeth Barry (c.1658–1713) included Cordelia and the frontispiece of Rowe's 1709 edition of Shakespeare shows her as Gertrude.*

LEFT *Anne Bracegirdle (c.1663–1748), one of the highest earning and most charismatic actresses of the age, performing at Drury Lane.*

RIGHT *Susanna Cibber (1714–55) as Cordelia in Nahum Tate's adaptation of* King Lear, *the version that held the stage until the mid nineteenth century.*

Shakespeare in the Eighteenth Century

The eighteenth century saw a remarkable expansion of interest in Shakespeare, as he was promoted, sometimes for political ends, as a writer of genius and as the National Poet, superior in skill to classical writers and past and present dramatists in Europe. The proliferation of editions shows the development of literary, and commercial, interest in Shakespeare.

ABOVE *Alexander Pope (1688–1744), whose six-volume edition of Shakespeare identified beautiful and ugly passages of language.*

PANEL FAR RIGHT *The popular actor Spranger Barry, seen here as Romeo, came to prominence playing Othello in Dublin.*

RIGHT *The 1769 Stratford Shakespeare Jubilee Rotunda, built on the banks of the Avon, where Garrick delivered his "Ode to Shakespeare".*

In 1709, the playwright Nicholas Rowe produced the first edited Collected Works, adding a recognizable apparatus to the plays: act and scene divisions, consistent entrances and exits in the texts and *dramatis personae*. Alexander Pope's edition of 1725 identified beautiful passages with an asterisk and dropped what he, as a poet, felt to be ugly passages to the foot of the page. Subsequent editors attempted greater objectivity but it was not until 1790 that Edmond Malone went back to the original texts and cleared away the more fanciful accretions. Many editions attempted to offer something new, such as Francis Hayman's beautiful illustrations in the first Oxford edition of 1744, or Samuel Johnson's critical preface in his edition of 1765. None, however, were concerned with Shakespeare in performance until John Bell's edition of 1773–4, which included cast lists from Drury Lane and Covent Garden and engravings of contemporary actors.

Bell's edition was dedicated to David Garrick, the greatest and most influential Shakespearian of the century, who became the manager of Drury Lane in 1747 and reformed stage practice, banning the audience from the stage and behind the scenes and abolishing the disruptive practice of half-price admission part way through an evening's show. His production innovations included new lighting and scenic effects, new costumes and the training of actors and a corps of dancers. His reputation, however, was based firmly on his

own acting skill that moved away from the prevailing opera-like declamatory style to something more naturalistic. He was renowned for his "start" of shock in *Richard III* and would reprise the moment in response to wild applause.

At the beginning of his career, Garrick performed in other dramatists' versions of Shakespeare – Tate's *Lear*, Cibber's *Richard III* – but began to create his own adaptations, reducing the plays to single plot lines (*A Midsummer Night's Dream* became, with musical additions, *The Fairies*). Such plays were short, but formed part of double or triple bills that were devised, in part, to compete with Covent Garden and also to give actors an opportunity to show their range in response to the audience's desire for variety.

Garrick was also a great enthusiast – he built a Temple of Shakespeare in his garden at Hampton on the Thames for his collection of memorabilia, his statue of Shakespeare (now in the British Museum) and his early editions. His greatest celebration of Shakespeare was the Stratford Shakespeare Jubilee of 1769, devised as three days of activities to dedicate the new town hall and a statue of Shakespeare (still to be seen on the corner of the building). His fame was such that his portraits, in and out of role, by artists such as Hogarth, Zoffany, Reynolds and Gainsborough, became best-selling prints and began the vogue for Shakespeare paintings that culminated at the end of the period in the Shakespeare

BACKGROUND *Garrick built a Temple of Shakespeare in the garden of his villa on the banks of the Thames at Hampton.*

OPPOSITE *"The Apotheosis of Garrick": Garrick is lifted heavenwards where Shakespeare waits to receive him. His earthly companions – actors and writers – bid him farewell.*

The most important and influential literary figure of the age, Johnson taught Garrick at Eidal, near Lichfield. They travelled to London together in 1737 and maintained a lifelong connection. In addition to his major edition of Shakespeare (1765) and his Dictionary (1755), which quoted extensively from Shakespeare, Johnson wrote prologues for the theatre and Shakespeare criticism, and assisted Charlotte Lennox, whose *Shakespeare Illustrated* of 1754 was the first published collection of Shakespeare's source material.

Gallery of John Boydell (1719–1804), an Alderman and three times Lord Mayor of London who commissioned the greatest artists to paint scenes from each play. He displayed the original works in London, but his plan to sell prints in Europe was wrecked by the French Revolution.

There were, of course, many fine actors in addition to Garrick, but in the close-knit world of the London theatre there was usually a connection to him. Charles Macklin (1699–1797), who helped prepare Garrick to play Lear, was a definitive Shylock turning the role from the prevailing comedy to tragedy. James Quin (1693–1766) was the favourite Falstaff, and Garrick wrote the epitaph for his tomb in Bath Abbey. The great tragic actress (and sister of John Philip and Charles Kemble) Sarah Siddons made her London debut for Garrick as Portia in 1775 and went on to become a crowd-drawing star.

At the same time, Shakespeare's plays also had a broader cultural influence. The preface to Horace Walpole's gothic novel, *Castle of Otranto*, acknowledged its debt to *Hamlet* and readers' growing familiarity with the texts generated popular parodies and poetry of the period is littered with Shakespeare quotations and allusions. Most were ephemeral, but Garrick's songs and verses from the Jubilee have endured – "The Mulberry Tree", "Warwickshire Will" and "Sweet Willy O" are still performed.

Shakespeare in the Nineteenth Century

At the beginning of the period, both Covent Garden and Drury Lane burned down and the size of the new theatres, each holding an audience of over 3,000, contributed to a new, large-scale and predominantly visual performance style that was evident in the work of the great actor-managers of the period: John Philip Kemble, nearing the end of his career, at Covent Garden and William Charles Macready in both houses.

FORGERY

Kemble was widely perceived as Garrick's successor and like him was a prodigious adaptor of Shakespeare's work. Macready, on the other hand, worked to restore the texts and was the first to abandon Tate's version of *Lear* and restore the role of the Fool.

King Charles' original Royal Patents, which, reinforced by the Licensing Act of 1737, had given the two theatres their monopoly of "legitimate" spoken drama, were effectively ended by the Theatres Act of 1843. This caused a mini flowering of Shakespeare productions, particularly at the newly refurbished

Haymarket Theatre, at Sadlers' Wells under the management of Samuel Phelps and at the Princesses Theatre under Charles Kean. Kean's father Edmund had been responsible for a new, influential, passionate style of acting that led the Romantic poet Samuel Taylor Coleridge to say, memorably, "To see him act is like reading Shakespeare by flashes of lightning". Ellen Terry's first professional appearance was with Charles' Kean's company, in 1854, when she was just seven, playing the Duke of York in *Richard III*. In the following four years, her Shakespearian roles included Mamillius, Prince Arthur, Fleance and Puck, which she performed for 200 consecutive nights. Following the retirement of Kean in 1859 and Phelps in 1862, the London Shakespeare revival faltered. This was partly due to the costs of the lavish production style that needed long runs to achieve profitability and partly because of the lack

During the period some people were driven to exploit Shakespeare's fame through very dubious means. The documents, deeds and letters with Shakespeare's signatures forged by William Ireland (1777–1835), above, were published by his father Samuel in 1795 and although exposed by Edmond Malone led to intense critical debate. Ireland also forged manuscript copies of *Lear* and *Hamlet* and three supposedly lost Shakespeare plays: *Vortigern and Rowena*, *Henry II* and *William the Conqueror*. More plausible were the forgeries of John Payne Collier (1789–1883), who made annotations to a Second Folio of Shakespeare's works (1632) and passed them off as authentic additions. In 1859, forensic tests revealed this and other documents in Collier's collections to be forgeries. Doubt remains about the status of documents in many public and private collections.

ABOVE *A silk favour using the Chandos portrait of Shakespeare that was issued for the Tercentenary celebrations of Shakespeare's birth.*

ABOVE *Charles Kean (1811–68) as Hamlet. Not the greatest actor, he was a very successful manager and directed Royal Theatricals at Windsor Castle.*

LEFT AND BACKGROUND *Drury Lane Theatre, shown here in 1808, burnt down the following year and was replaced by the present building. It opened in 1812 with a performance of Hamlet and a special prologue delivered by Lord Byron.*

RIGHT *Edmund Kean's original, dynamic acting style – here as Othello – was appreciated and recorded by the Romantics.*

ABOVE (TOP) *Henry Irving and Ellen Terry in* Much Ado About Nothing *at the Lyceum in 1882. The historical and archaeological details of such sets ("pictorial Shakespeare") were expensive to create and time-consuming to erect and change.*

ABOVE *Ellen Terry first performed with Kean's company at the Princesses Theatre in 1854. Here, aged nine, she plays Mamillius in* The Winter's Tale.

RIGHT *Sir Henry Irving, the first actor to be honoured with a knighthood, was accorded a funeral in Westminster Abbey.*

of actors experienced in the classical repertoire, but largely because of the increasing popularity of touring, particularly to the newly opened, well-equipped, provincial theatres, that was facilitated by the fast developing railway system. The situation persisted until Henry Irving (1838–1905) took over the lease of the Lyceum in the Strand in 1878.

With Ellen Terry (1847–1928) as his leading lady, he developed a distinctive house style and strove for an aesthetically appealing naturalism. He treated Shakespeare plays as if they were historical books to be illustrated with accurate period scenery, often designed by artists of some repute such as Alma Tadema, Burne-Jones and Ford Madox Brown, lavishly detailed period costume and atmospheric music (Arthur Sullivan wrote the overture and incidental music for their *Macbeth* in 1888). The effects were enhanced by the innovation of darkening the auditorium and lighting the area behind it to obtain three-dimensional images, and resisting the introduction of electricity because the use of gas and limelight further reinforced the sense of creating pictures.

There were two victims of such lavish spectacle: the text, which had to be cut to accommodate the time-consuming business of erecting, dismantling and changing the sets (Irving

cut 1,507 lines from *King Lear* for example, about 40 per cent of the play), and a naturalistic acting style. Actors could be dwarfed by the scale of the set and the complexity of their costumes and compensated by developing large-scale, "pictorial" acting in which poses were struck and held – posture was as important as gesture and beautiful, but quite unnatural, tableaux were created. It was two-dimensional acting set against three-dimensional sets. It dominated influential productions of *Romeo and Juliet*, *Hamlet*, *Much Ado About Nothing* and *Macbeth* and survived well into the twentieth century, influencing early cinema and opera.

Shakespeare Today

T he story of Shakespearian theatre in the twentieth century begins and ends, in Britain at least, with attempts to recreate authentic, original staging, a possible reaction to elaborate design that privileged the visual experience over the language of the plays. There is a continued distinction (evident in the academic study of Shakespeare, too) between those who wish to disinter the past and those who, like the Royal Shakespeare Company, wish to make Shakespeare accessible and relevant to new audiences in new spaces.

The efforts of the actor-manager William Poel (1852–1934) to recreate a replica Elizabethan theatre with appropriate costumes and acting style was a direct response to the enduring influence of Irving's Victorian spectacle, evident in the management of Her/His Majesty's theatre by Sir Herbert Beerbohm Tree from 1897 to 1915. It included such "historical" additions as the signing of Magna Carta in *King John* and real rabbits to *A Midsummer Night's Dream*. Similarly, Sam Wanamaker's great project to recreate Shakespeare's Globe on the South Bank, which opened in 1996, is in part a reaction to the design concepts that frequently dominated productions on the larger stages. It followed in the footsteps of the Royal Shakespeare Company and the Royal National Theatre who have both created more intimate playing spaces, such as the Swan Theatre that opened in Stratford in 1986.

Between these points, authenticity was also sought in other forms: the use of "authentic" rather than cut or adapted texts begun again by Poel in his production of the First Quarto *Hamlet*, and all male productions, particularly of *As You Like It*

(by Ben Greet in 1920, Clifford Williams for the National Theatre in 1967 and Cheek by Jowl's production that toured extensively in 1991–2). Instead of recreating original staging, however, many directors have striven for a different sort of integrity – contemporary relevance rather than historical accuracy. Sir Barry Jackson, founder of the Birmingham Rep and Director of the Shakespeare Memorial Theatre (the RSC's predecessor) 1945–8, was the first in the twentieth century to stage Shakespeare in modern dress. This included a *Hamlet* "in plus fours", as they were known in 1925, and a 1928 *Macbeth* set in the First World War. Many productions subsequently sought to make the plays accessible through the use of neither historical nor completely modern costume and set, but through the choice of a period that was familiar to audiences, perhaps through television exposure, that retained elements of status, class, religion and gender relationships which accorded with some of the original structures. The RSC's *Merry Wives of Windsor* (1985) set in the early 1950s, and *Two Gentlemen of Verona* (1994) set in the 1930s and using Cole Porter songs worked very well. Indeed, the 1930s has become

ABOVE William Poel, who founded the Elizabethan Stage Society and explored original setting.

RIGHT Sir Barry Jackson (1879–1961) founded the Birmingham Repertory Theatre in 1913 and explored Shakespeare in modern dress.

BELOW Sir Herbert Beerbohm Tree (1853–1917), here as Richard III, whose spectacular Shakespearian productions attracted huge audiences to Her/His Majesty's Theatre.

LAURENCE OLIVIER
c.1907–89

An actor-manager and star in the tradition of Garrick and Irving, Olivier is an integral part of twentieth-century Shakespeare. His performances on stage in London in the 1930s, often with John Gielgud, and particularly at the Old Vic under Tyrone Guthrie and in the 1940s with Ralph Richardson, demonstrated his range and made him a star. This experience, his successful Shakespeare films and some strong seasons at Stratford made him the obvious choice to head the National Theatre in its temporary home at the Old Vic from 1962 to 1973. Ill-health prevented him heading the company in its permanent home, but the largest theatre in the complex is named the Olivier.

FAR LEFT The American actor Sam Wanamaker (1919–93), who was the inspiration of the reconstructed Globe theatre.

LEFT The RSC's 1994 Two Gentlemen of Verona, staged in the Swan Theatre, was set in the 1930s and used songs of the period.

The original Shakespeare Memorial Theatre (SMT) in Stratford, instigated at the Shakespeare Tercentenary Celebrations in 1864, opened in 1879 and performed summer festivals until destroyed by fire in 1926. Its shell now houses the Swan Theatre, constructed in 1986, and a display space. Peter Hall took on the management of the replacement 1930s' SMT in 1960, renaming it the Royal Shakespeare Theatre and forming the Royal Shakespeare Company the following year. The main theatre was transformed by a major three-year construction project and reopened in 2011 with stalls and two galleries wrapped around three sides of a thrust stage. While the work was undertaken, the company used the newly constructed Courtyard Theatre and this has been retained as a third venue. Hall and the artistic directors who followed him – Trevor Nunn, Terry Hands, Adrian Noble, Michael Boyd and Gregory Doran – have created the most influential and productive Shakespeare company that attracts the greatest actors and directors. Through its touring programme, regular performances in London and residencies in Newcastle upon Tyne and universities and performance centres across the USA, the RSC has a national and international reach. It is still at heart an ensemble company that encourages new talent.

ABOVE LEFT *Janet Dale and Lindsay Duncan in The Merry Wives of Windsor (RSC, 1987) set in the 1950s.*

ABOVE RIGHT *Tamora, Queen of the Goths, pleads with Titus (Laurence Olivier) for the life of her sons in Peter Brook's 1955 production that rescued the reputation of the play.*

PANEL FAR RIGHT *The re-designed Royal Shakespeare Theatre, on the banks of the Avon in Stratford, was opened in 2011. The original was designed by Elisabeth Scott.*

BELOW *Peter Brook's influential "white box" A Midsummer Night's Dream (RSC, 1970), with Alan Howard as Oberon and Sara Kestelman as Titania, that peeled away athe pretty, romantic accretions of previous productions.*

a commonplace setting for history plays (*Richard III* at the RNT, 1990) and *Measure for Measure*.

Jackson was the first to employ Peter Brook at Stratford and Brook's innovative work, that combined simpler staging with a relevance to the tougher spirit of the age, makes him, for many, the greatest director of the century. His *Titus Andronicus* with Laurence Olivier and Vivien Leigh (1955) rescued the play from critical and performance neglect; his *King Lear* with Paul Scofield (1962), created after discussion with Jan Kott, the influential author of *Shakespeare our Contemporary* (1964), emphasized the cruelty and harshness of the play world and his own; and his "white box" production of *A Midsummer Night's Dream* (1970) peeled away the pretty and romantic accretions of the play and exploited the skills of circus.

Off stage, major developments have occurred in the editing of Shakespeare with significant editions from Arden, Cambridge and, most influentially, the Oxford Complete Works (the basis of the Norton edition in the States). The Royal Shakespeare Company has commissioned a new Collected Works based, uniquely, on the First Folio. In addition to re-assessing the texts and making editorial choice explicit, many new editions respond to the most significant academic shift of the period – to performance studies and criticism. A number of publishers produce schools' editions of Shakespeare with tasks and activities designed to engage the young for whom, in the UK, Shakespeare is a compulsory part of the curriculum.

The most recent textual development is the provision of on-line editions with some, such as the British Library's collection, available in facsimile. It is electronic Shakespeare that looks set to dominate the twenty-first century, as theatre and library collections become available on-line and the quality of available criticism improves. The last ten years have seen a revival of Shakespeare biography that looks set to continue, although without further historical discoveries this is likely to be speculative or a re-arrangement of known facts rather than anything new.

On stage, the trend is for "theming" or grouping (and thus selling) the plays, finding new connections for new audiences. From 2006 the RSC staged the entire canon, offering audiences the chance to see rarely performed works and to marvel at Shakespeare's range. For critics this provided an opportunity to continue to interrogate Shakespeare's role in high and low culture and his significance for the heritage industry. Like Garrick's 1769 Shakespeare Jubilee, this festival focused attention on the town of the playwright's birth, but the story of twentieth- and twenty-first-century Shakespeare, far from being confined to Stratford, is one of proliferation into every corner of the world and into new media with an international reach.

Shakespeare Around the World

Shakespeare himself never travelled abroad, but his work left England early – in 1607, aboard the East India Company's ship Dragon where, off the coast of Sierra Leone, Captain William Keeling's crew performed *Hamlet* and *Richard II*. *Hamlet* was performed at sea again the following year, its function, as Keeling explained, was "to keep my people from idleness and unlawful games, or sleep".

ABOVE *Medals struck in Argentina to commemorate Shakespeare's 400th birthday.*

RIGHT *The French actress Sarah Bernhardt (1844–1923) in Marcel Schwob's 1899 adaptation of Hamlet.*

BELOW *The early days of the Stratford Festival in Stratford, Ontario, Canada in 1953.*

BELOW RIGHT *Welcome Msomi's Zulu adaptaton of Macbeth, Umabatha, was first performed in Natal in 1972 and has since been presented all around the world.*

At the same time, professional actors were visiting much of Europe, but little is known about their repertoires and touring largely ceased during the Thirty Years War (1618–48). The main proliferation occurred from the eighteenth century onwards as "Shakespeare" travelled abroad in a range of guises and along a variety of routes. It left with British soldiers garrisoned in Canada after 1763; via the English education system to the former colonies and the Commonwealth; to Japan as a *Hamlet* quotation, "Neither a borrower nor a lender be", in Samuel Smiles' Victorian *Self Help*; but mainly through

performance and, to the non-English speaking world, through translation.

The earliest spread was into Europe. Voltaire's partial translation of 1733 was followed in France by Le Tourneur's complete translation in 1776. *Julius Caesar* was translated into German in 1741, the first Italian translation, of the same play, occurred in 1756, and *Hamlet* was translated into Spanish in 1772. *Hamlet* was first performed in Swedish in Gothenburg in 1787 and translated into Russian in 1828. The major, and long-enduring, German association with Shakespeare began with August Schlegel's translation of 16 plays in 1797, a task completed by Ludwig Tieck and others in 1832. In 1752, the first Shakespeare play was performed in New York – *Richard III* – and *Henry IV* was the first known performance in Australia in 1800.

The enthusiasm for Shakespeare worldwide has taken a number of forms. Some countries have established

VOLTAIRE

(FRANÇOIS-MARIE AROUET)

c.1694–1778

The French playwright, writer and philosopher Voltaire visited England in the late 1720s. While he expressed admiration for Shakespeare, his less than appreciative comments on the stage and its audiences and his subsequent translations (turning "To be or not to be" into French alexandrines, for example) irritated increasingly bardolatrous English Shakespearians. Elizabeth Montagu's influential and popular 1769 *Essay on the Writings and Genius of Shakespeare* offered a witty defence of Shakespeare against Voltaire.

formal associations, usually driven by academics: Germany's Deutsche Shakespeare-Gesellschaft, established in 1864 (the tercentenary of Shakespeare's birth); the Shakespeare Association of America, founded in 1923; the Shakespeare Association of Japan, formed in 1962; and the Australian and New Zealand Shakespeare Association, established in 1990. The International Shakespeare Association, founded in 1974 and administered in Stratford-upon-Avon, works with national associations to organize themed world congresses that reflect local culture and performance in addition to "academic" Shakespeare. Washington (1976), Stratford-upon-Avon (1981), Berlin (1986), Tokyo (1991), Los Angeles (1996), Valencia (2001) and Brisbane (2006) have all hosted congresses.

Some proliferation has taken a more concrete form, such as the collections of the Folger Shakespeare Library in Washington DC, or the replicas of Shakespeare's theatres – a Globe in Tokyo and a Blackfriars in Stanton, Virginia – or a dedicated theatre, such as the one in Stratford, Ontario, Canada, founded in 1953 and directed by Tyrone Guthrie, or a replica of Anne Hathaway's Cottage in Victoria, BC in Canada.

It would be wrong, however, to see Shakespeare's worldwide proliferation as nothing more than the replication of English texts and performances into new languages and new venues. His work has been adapted and re-presented to suit specific cultural and social needs. The earliest performance of Shakespeare in Japan was a Kabuki adaptation of the *Merchant of Venice* in 1885. In 1934, the Comedie-Française production of *Coriolanus* as a fascist attack on democracy led to riots; the 1935 Stalinist-approved production of the same play in Moscow showed Coriolanus as the enemy of the people; the Nazis approved of Coriolanus as a strong leader so the play was banned in post-war, occupied Germany until 1953. Janet Suzman directed an *Othello* in Johannesburg in 1988 that directly reflected apartheid with the black African actor John Kani in the title role and Iago presented as the white supremacist Eugene Terre Blanche. It should be noted, too, that "world Shakespeare" has influenced the home product: Tomasso Salvini's passionate Othello, performed in London in 1875 *in Italian*, set new standards of tragic playing, and Sarah Bernhardt as Hamlet in London in 1899 was much admired. Perhaps the most influential and far-reaching overseas engagement with Shakespeare has been neither on the page nor the stage but through the medium of film.

In 1885, Henry Clay Folger gave a facsimile of the First Folio to his wife Emily. Four years later, he purchased an original copy of the Fourth Folio and subsequently used the wealth that he acquired as President of the Standard Oil Company to amass the greatest Shakespeare collection in the world that now includes 79 copies of the First Folio as well as quartos and memorabilia. The Folgers gave their collection to the American nation in 1928 and the Library in Washington attracts visitors from all over the world.

Shakespeare on Film

54

Shakespeare was quickly appropriated by the new medium as motion pictures developed from the experiments of Edison and the Lumiere brothers in the early 1890s. While Shakespeare provided kudos and cultural capital to the emerging form, the new medium itself appealed to the entrepreneurial instincts of the major theater practitioners.

Shakespeare on film has its origins in, and has largely been sustained by, the "actor-manager" tradition that shifted from one performance arena to another. The backbone of screen Shakespeare has been directors who are also fine stage actors – Olivier, Welles, Branagh, McKellen – the "actor-director" tradition and the link between theatre and film performance has been strong. Scholars argue about the relationship between stage and screen of the first surviving film – a segment of *King John* by Sir Herbert Beerbohm Tree – as the two opened simultaneously in 1899 but the film, which used the stage costumes, clearly reflected Tree's work at Her Majesty's Theatre. The short films made by Frank Benson's company, of which only the 1911 *Richard III* survives, were actually shot on stage at Stratford. The postural and gestural extravagance, a staple of late nineteenth-century stage acting, was not inappropriate for the demands of black-and-white, silent films. These early pieces, plus *Hamlet* of 1913 with Sir

Johnston Forbes Robertson, established the enduring practice, in the UK at least, of Shakespeare on film as the province of stage actors. As the medium developed, the lavish "pictorial realism" of the sets of the late Victorian stage could be reproduced and exploited more effectively than within the confines of a theatre.

Similar developments were evident throughout Europe. As early as 1900, the duel scene from Sarah Bernhardt's stage *Hamlet* was filmed in France, while in Italy lavish productions of *Julius Caesar* and *Marcantonio e Cleopatra* were recorded in 1908 and 1913. Amongst the most innovative early silent films was the German production of *Hamlet* with the Danish actress Asta Nielsen in the title role. This offered a psychological interpretation of the play with Nielsen – a woman – in love with Horatio.

The development of Shakespeare on film in the United States was more complex. D. W. Griffiths used English

ORSON WELLES
c.(1915–85)

Welles acquired his reputation as an innovative, even provocative Shakespearian with his New York stage production of a modern-dress, anti-fascist *Julius Caesar* in 1937. After the success of *Citizen Kane*, he turned to film Shakespeare with adaptations of *Macbeth* (1948), *Othello* (1952), and *Chimes at Midnight* (released in some countries as *Falstaff*) in 1966. He starred in each and the latter, a version of the *Henry IV* plays, is regarded as his greatest achievement and a sensitive exploration of the relationship between Prince Hal and the fat knight.

ABOVE *D. W. Griffiths' 1916 silent Hollywood* Macbeth *with Sir Herbert Beerbohm Tree and Constance Collier.*

PANEL RIGHT *Orson Welles as Falstaff in* Chimes at Midnight.

BELOW *Douglas Fairbanks and Mary Pickford in the 1929* The Taming of the Shrew, *the first full-length Shakespeare "talkie".*

BELOW RIGHT *The Mechanicals in Reinhardt's 1935* A Midsummer Night's Dream, *with James Cagney, second left, as Bottom.*

and American stage actors for silent films of *Macbeth* and *Lear*. Hollywood used established screen actors in the first full-length talkie – the 1929 *Taming of the Shrew* directed by Sam Taylor with Douglas Fairbanks and Mary Pickford in the leading roles. The taming sequences were the occasion for carefully choreographed slapstick humour that reflected Taylor's background and expertise in silent comedy. Kate attacked Petruccio with a stool and, far from being cowed or submissive at the end, concluded the film with an exaggerated conspiratorial wink to the audience.

Max Reinhardt's 1935 *A Midsummer Night's Dream* combined Hollywood casting (Dick Powell as Lysander, Mickey Rooney as Puck, James Cagney as Bottom) with European cultural traditions. Reinhardt had an international reputation as a stage director in Berlin and Munich and his innovative approach to Shakespeare transferred well on to the screen. While he used Mendelssohn's famous *Dream* music, arranged by Korngold, this was far from the conventional film that such a traditional musical choice might imply and still surprises, even shocks, with the Gothic eroticism of Oberon's all male fairies. It was far removed, too, from a stage performance and exploited the monochrome of the new medium with striking effects of shadow and moonlight. It may be seen as the precursor of the "art house" Shakespeare films of much later in the century, such as the *Tempests* of Derek Jarman (1980), Paul Mazursky (1982) and Peter Greenaway (*Prospero's Books*, 1991). Even when colour was available to them, some subsequent directors chose to film in black and white. Much of the strength and tension, and indeed seriousness, of Olivier's *Hamlet* (1948), Orson Welles' *Othello* (1952) and Peter Brook's *King Lear* (1971) is achieved through an interplay of light and dark.

Olivier's first Shakespeare film was as Orlando in Paul Czinner's 1936 *As You Like It*, but neither it nor George Cukor's *Romeo and Juliet* from the same year (which also used British actors – Leslie Howard and Norma Shearer)

was successful at the box office. Both lacked Reinhardt's flair and were ponderous, reverential cinema. Olivier's own trilogy of Shakespeare films was much more dynamic while each acknowledged its theatrical origins. The first, *Henry V* from 1943, began with a view of Elizabethan London and the Chorus delivered at the Globe Theatre before moving to the fields of France (and, in so doing, drawing on the patriotic impulses of the time); *Hamlet* reflected Olivier's stage experience in the role; and the third, the faux-medieval *Richard III* of 1955, gave a script credit to the eighteenth-century text adapters Colley Cibber and David Garrick. Orson Welles also drew on his experience as a precocious actor and director and translated his powerful Shakespeare stage persona into a trilogy of enduring films.

TOP LEFT *Sven Gade's 1920 silent film of* Hamlet *with actress Asta Nielsen in the title role.*

TOP RIGHT *Orson Welles in the title role of his black and white 1952* Othello.

ABOVE *Laurence Olivier's first Shakespeare film appearance was as Orlando in* As You Like It, *1936.*

PANEL FAR RIGHT *Max Reinhardt (centre) discussing the set design for* A Midsummer Night's Dream *with Anton Grot and William Dieterle in 1935.*

RIGHT *Laurence Olivier in the title role of his patriotic film* Henry V *of 1943.*

Reinhardt came to fame at the Deutsches Theater in Berlin where he staged large-scale lavish Shakespeare productions, including 12 *Dreams*. This popular style of work was replicated in London and elsewhere in Europe, but he also engaged in smaller, experimental stage work (*Hamlet* and *King Lear*, for example) and non-Shakespearian films in Germany. As an Austrian Jew, his position became impossible and he moved to the USA in 1933 where he worked in commercial theatre and film.

Shakespeare on Film
STRETCHING THE BOUNDARIES

Shortly after Olivier and Welles' influential trilogies, Shakespeare on film began to spread significantly beyond the English-speaking world and Europe. Not surprisingly perhaps, given the familiarity of their plots and the perception that they possessed universal significance, the most popular vehicles for such cultural journeys were the tragedies.

RIGHT *Paul Scofield as Lear (right) with Harry Andrews in Peter Brook's bleak black and white film of 1971 that drew on his 1962 stage production for the RSC.*

PANEL RIGHT *Kenneth Branagh as Hamlet in his 1997 film.*

BELOW LEFT *Grigori Kozintsev's Russian Hamlet with Innokenti Smoktunovski as Hamlet and Anastasia Vertinskaya as Ophelia.*

BELOW RIGHT *Akira Kurosawa's Throne of Blood presented Macbeth as a samurai warrior.*

FAR RIGHT *Elizabeth Taylor as Kate in Franco Zeffirelli's colourful Taming of the Shrew in 1966. The film benefited from the off-screen relationship between Taylor and Richard Burton who played Petruchio.*

In Russia, Sergei Yutkevich's *Othello* (1955) used Boris Pasternak's translation of Shakespeare and Katchachurian's music to create a powerful and more romantic rendering of the story than was common in the west. Nine years later Grigori Kozintsev's *Hamlet* presented a hero – played by the stage actor Innokenti Smoktunovski – who remains, for many, the definitive Dane. The decision to deliver the monologues as voice-overs gave added power to the representation. Kozintsev's choice of black and white for *Hamlet* and the *King Lear* that followed in 1969 gave both films an austerity (and *Lear* a desolation) that contrasted with the colourful and sensual lusciousness of Franco Zeffirelli's Shakespeare films that, at the same time, were appealing to young audiences in Britain and the US.

In Japan, Akira Kurosawa drew on very different traditions of acting and film-making when he adapted three Shakespeare tragedies. *Macbeth* (*The Throne of Blood*, 1957), *Hamlet* (*The Bad Sleep Well*, 1963) and *King Lear* (*Ran*, 1985) were heavily influenced by Kabuki and Noh theatre and many feel that

through his use of unexpected colour, costume and setting Kurosawa created the most visually exciting Shakespeare-inspired films.

Throughout the period, successful stage productions were being transferred to the cinema screen. This is a commercial and artistic development that has left records of some great performances: Olivier and Maggie Smith in *Othello* (Stuart Burge, 1965, a version of the National Theatre production); Peter Hall's *A Midsummer Night's Dream* of 1969 based on his RSC production with a cast that included Diana Rigg, Helen Mirren and Judi Dench; Peter Brook's particularly dark 1971 *King Lear* starring Paul Scofield and based on the production for the RSC of 1962; Trevor Nunn's *Macbeth* with Judi Dench and Ian McKellen of 1979 based on the small-scale, in-the-round, RSC production; and the same director's film version of his RSC *Othello* with Willard White in the

KENNETH BRANAGH
1960–

A Shakespearian in the Olivier tradition (and strongly influenced by him) who achieved success with the RSC, Branagh founded the Renaissance Company and directed popular Shakespeare films clearly informed by his stage work. He took the lead in his screen versions of *Henry V* (1989), *Much Ado About Nothing* (1993) and a full text *Hamlet* (1997) and played Berowne in a musical version of *Love's Labour's Lost* (2000), in each case attracting the highest calibre stage and film actors to join him. He played Iago in Oliver Parker's *Othello* opposite Laurence Fishburne and continues to explore the potential of Shakespeare on film.

PANEL FAR RIGHT *Franco Zeffirelli directed some of the most visually stylish Shakespeare films.*

RIGHT *Baz Luhrmann's 1996 updating of the setting and casting of Leonardo diCaprio attracted young audiences to* Romeo and Juliet.

ABOVE *The 1930s setting of Ian McKellen (here in the title role) and Richard Loncraine's* Richard III *gave a twentieth-century political relevance to the plot.*

RIGHT *Kenneth Branagh's cross-Atlantic casting (including here Denzel Washington and Michael Keaton) gave* Much Ado About Nothing, *1993, wide box-office appeal.*

FAR RIGHT *Anthony Hopkins as Titus in Julie Taymor's eclectic film of 1999.*

title role and McKellen as Iago. While not all have translated well – Olivier's large-scale acting seems inappropriate for the screen (and his "blacking up" as Othello now very unfashionable) – other theatre off-shoots endure effectively. Ian McKellen and Richard Loncraine's *Richard III* of 1995 which developed from ideas first explored in Richard Eyre's Royal National Theatre production is less a filmed record than a re-working, with significant textual cuts, an extension of the 1930s setting and the use of familiar London buildings as well as location settings such as Shoreham airport and Rye harbour. And the films of Kenneth Branagh, a pillar of the actor-manager-director tradition, have their roots in his own performances and in ensemble stage work.

Recent films have travelled some distance from the stage and reached new audiences. Baz Luhrmann's *William Shakespeare's Romeo + Juliet* (1996) relocated and updated the story to a media-obsessed US and in the casting of Leonardo diCaprio and Claire Danes appealed particularly to the young. Julie Taymor's *Titus* (1999 with Anthony Hopkins and Jessica Lange) achieved what many had thought impossible – the filming of Shakespeare's most violent play – and in choosing an eclectic mix of Roman and modern costume and set gave the bloody play a contemporary relevance. Both are fine examples of Shakespeare's sustained popularity, adaptability and enduring power to communicate through new media.

The Italian director first encountered Shakespeare through a copy of John Singer Sargent's portrait of Ellen Terry as Lady Macbeth, hanging on his English tutor's wall. Like Branagh a great Shakespeare populariser, Zeffirelli's films of *Romeo and Juliet* (1968, following his successful 1960 Old Vic stage version with Judi Dench as Juliet), *The Taming of the Shrew* (1966, with Richard Burton and Elizabeth Taylor) and *Hamlet* (1990, with Mel Gibson) were visually stunning and attracted new audiences to the classic works.

Shakespeare in Other Media

Shakespeare – the man, his reputation, his works on page and stage – has been used (some would say abused) in a remarkable range of media. The proliferation of his image, which had begun in 1710 with the Tonson publishers' use of the Chandos portrait as its trademark, dates from the period of the 1769 Stratford Shakespeare Jubilee when Garrick was presented with a medal featuring Shakespeare's head.

PANEL RIGHT *"The wall" in English National Opera's production of Britten's* A Midsummer Night's Dream, *2004.*

BELOW *Shakespeare has been used to advertise beer, cigars, breakfast cereals and here "Draper's Ink".*

BOTTOM LEFT *In Jane Austen's* Mansfield Park, *Mr Crawford entertained Fanny and Lady Bertram by reading passages from* Henry VIII: *"He could always light, at will, on the best scene, or the best speeches".*

BOTTOM RIGHT *John Everett Millais'"Ophelia", 1852, one of the most popular Pre-Raphaelite paintings.*

Garrick conducted affairs with a wand crafted from the mulberry tree supposedly planted by Shakespeare, wore a waistcoat in rainbow Shakespeare-Jubilee colours and addressed audiences who were wearing Jubilee ribbons and were keen to purchase souvenir images in wood, pottery and on handkerchiefs. In the nineteenth century, the Stratford brewery Flowers (run by a family who were immensely generous patrons of the theatre) used a picture of Shakespeare on its beer mats and bottle labels, and Shakespeare has been used more recently to promote tobacco, a breakfast cereal, a photocopier, Coca-Cola and Carling Black Label.

Shakespeare's influence on other writers may be seen as a more legitimate appropriation. His plots and characters are evident in the work of major novelists such as Jane Austen (particularly in *Mansfield Park*), Charles Dickens, Virginia Woolf (*Orlando* draws on *As You Like It*), and also poets as diverse as William Wordsworth and W. H. Auden and dramatists of the likes of Anton Chekhov and Henrik Ibsen (who both use *Hamlet*), Sheridan (in *The Critic*) and George Bernard Shaw, who advised Ellen Terry on playing Imogen, re-wrote the last act of *Cymbeline* and whose last

work, for puppets, was *Shakes versus Shaw* in 1949.

More recognizable, however, are the less mediated or manipulated transitions of Shakespeare's characters from one art form to another. Explicitly Shakespearian, for example, are Hogarth's portrait of Garrick as Richard III, or the Pre-Raphaelites' exploration of moral problems, as seen in Holman Hunt's paintings of scenes from *The Two Gentlemen of Verona* and *Measure for Measure*. Their interest in Shakespeare's heroines as exemplified in Rossetti's paintings of Ophelia, Lady Macbeth and Mariana and – perhaps the most famous picture – Millais' "Ophelia" (1852) showing her drowning. In 1964, Picasso celebrated the quartercentenary of Shakespeare's birth with 12 drawings of *Hamlet*. As well as being inspired by the plays, in each case the artist also benefits from the viewers' knowledge of the subject matter.

But such shared knowledge can also be a handicap, particularly with works for a new stage medium. In addition to the quality of music or dance, a performance may be judged by its distance from its source or the degree to which it illuminates the original. It is easy to deride the early, semi-operatic adaptations (the singing and dancing male witches in Davenant's *Macbeth*, for example) or the nineteenth-century

PYOTR ILYICH TCHAIKOVSKY
1840–93

travesties and burlesques of *Hamlet* rendered into comic rhyming couplets. Best received have been the translations into new media that have retained mood as well as basic plot or character. Verdi's *Otello* (1887) and *Falstaff* (1893) are enduringly popular, not least because they retain and explore the tone – tragic in one, comic in the other – of their source material. Similarly, the ballet versions of *Romeo and Juliet* that use Prokofiev's music (there have been at least six, choreographed by Lavrovsky, 1940; Ashton, 1955; Cranko, 1958; MacMillan, 1965; Neumeier, 1974 and Nureyev, 1977) work because they exploit and enhance the tragic tone as well as the plot of the original. The musical version of the same play, *West Side Story* (stage 1957 and film 1961), remains a powerful work because, in addition to its skillful updating to immigrant communities in New York, its music and lyrics (Bernstein and Sondheim) and dance (Robbins) support and complement Shakespeare's plot.

Just as Shakespeare himself drew heavily on the work of others for the basis of his plots, so now creative people, worldwide, exploit his familiarity and fame to craft new works in new media.

PANEL RIGHT *Robert Helpmann rehearsing the title role in his one-act* Hamlet *ballet that he created for Sadler's Wells in 1942.*

ABOVE LEFT *The opening night of* West Side Story, *based on* Romeo and Juliet, *on Broadway, in 1957.*

ABOVE RIGHT *Rudolph Nureyev rehearsing with Merle Park in* Romeo and Juliet, *which he devised to Prokofiev's music in 1977.*

LEFT *Placido Domingo in the title role of Verdi's* Otello, *which was composed in 1887.*

Russians have long been attracted to the tragic romanticism of Shakespeare, particularly *Hamlet*, which influenced Pushkin, Turgenev and Dostoevsky. Tchaikovsky wrote orchestral versions of *The Tempest* (1873), *Hamlet* (1888) and *Romeo and Juliet* (1869, rev. 1870 and 1880) and incidental music for *Hamlet* in 1891. His *Romeo and Juliet* was choreographed as a ballet in 1937 but is less well known than Prokofiev's. The one-act *Hamlet* ballet, created by Robert Helpmann (who danced the title role with Margot Fonteyn as Ophelia) for Sadler's Wells in 1942, fused Tchaikovsky's music with an imaginative, circular dance interpretation that opened with lines from the play:

"For in that sleep of death,
what dreams may come
When we have shuffled
off this mortal coil
Must give us pause."

The action began and ended with Hamlet's body being carried to his grave by hooded monks.

Year	SHAKESPEARE	NATIONAL EVENTS	INTERNATIONAL EVENTS
1564	• Birth of William Shakespeare, baptised 26 April	• Birth of Christopher Marlowe. • Elizabeth I elevated Robert Dudley to the peerage as the Earl of Leicester.	• John Hawkins' makes his second voyage to the New World. • Galileo Galilei born. • John Calvin dies.
1567		• Mary, Queen of Scots imprisoned on 15 May. She abdicates on 24 July, and her son becomes King James VI of Scotland. • Red Lion, the first purpose-built public theatre, opened in Stepney.	• The Dutch revolt against Spanish rule. • John Hawkins begins his third voyage, this time his journeys take him to Africa and Spanish America.
1568	• John Shakespeare made bailiff of Stratford.	• Mary, Queen of Scots escapes from prison and is defeated at Langside. She flees to England, where she is imprisoned by Elizabeth I at Fotheringay Castle.	
1572		• Birth of Ben Jonson.	• St Bartholomew's Day massacre – French Protestants massacred by French Catholics in Paris, 24 August.
1573	• Birth of Henry Wriothesley, Earl of Southampton, Shakespeare's patron.	• Elizabeth I gives Robert Devereaux, Earl of Essex, the right to colonize Ulster. • Sir Francis Drake returns to England from America with treasure he has plundered from the Spanish. • Birth of Inigo Jones. (d. 1652)	• The Franciscan order arrives in Florida.
1576	• James Burbage, Richard Burbage's father, builds The Theatre at Shoreditch.		• Spanish sack Antwerp. The Dutch provinces unite against Spain with the Treaty of Ghent. • The Earl of Essex dies.
1577		• Holinshed publishes The Chronicles of England, Scotland and Ireland.	• Sir Francis Drake begins his around the world journey in his ship, the Golden Hind.
1579	• Death of Shakespeare's sister, Anne.	• John Fletcher born. (d. 1625)	• Sir Francis Drake stakes claim of New Albion (California) for England.
1580	• Birth of Shakespeare's brother, Edmund.	• Thomas Middleton born. (d. 1627)	• Sir Francis Drake returns to England gloriously.
1582	• Marriage to Anne Hathaway, November.		
1583	• Birth of Shakespeare's first child, Susanna.	• Philip Massinger born. (d. 1640)	• Galileo discovers the principle governing the motion of the pendulum. • Sir Humphrey Gilbert launches second voyage to America, where he discovers and explores Newfoundland. He is lost at sea in September.
1585	• Birth of Shakespeare's twins, Hamnet and Judith.	• War with Spain begins and continues until 1604.	• First British settlement in North America established on Roanoke Island, in what is now North Carolina. • Elizabeth I concludes a treaty of alliance with the Dutch.
1587	• Rose Theatre built by Henslowe on Bankside.	• Mary, Queen of Scots executed.	• Second expedition to Roanoke Island by John White. He left his family there while he returned to England for supplies. On his return three years later, the colony had vanished. • Sir Francis Drake defeats the Spanish fleet at Cadiz. • Virginia Dare born in Roanoke colony, the first English child born in North America.
1588		• Spanish Armada defeated. • Death of Robert Dudley, Earl of Leicester.	
1590		• James VI of Scotland marries Anne of Denmark. • Edmund Spenser publishes first three books of The Faerie Queen.	• John White's relief expedition back to Roanoke finds no trace of the colonists.
1590–1	• *The Two Gentlemen of Verona* • *The Taming of the Shrew*		
1591	• *Henry VI, Part 2* • *Henry VI, Part 3*	• Tea is first drunk in England.	• Robert Devereux, Earl of Essex leads an expedition in France to support King Henri IV.
1592	• *Henry VI, Part 1* • *Titus Andronicus*	• Plague in London. Closes the theatres for two years.	
1593	• Composition of the sonnets begins. Continues until 1603.	• Christopher Marlowe killed in a brawl outside a pub in Deptford. • Penalties are proposed for people who refuse to attend Church of England services and to make it a crime to attend Catholic religious services.	
1592–3	• *Richard III* • *Venus and Adonis*		
1593–4	• *The Rape of Lucrece*		
1594	• *The Comedy of Errors*	• James VI of Scotland's first son, Henry, is born. • A three-year period of dire harvests begins. • Death of Thomas Kyd. (b. 1558)	• Henry of Navarre crowned Henry IV of France.
1594–5	• *Love's Labour's Lost*		
1595	• Shakespeare's name appears as a joint payee of the Lord Chamberlain's Men for their performances at court. • Swan Theatre built by Langley on Bankside. • *Richard II* • *Romeo and Juliet* • *A Midsummer Night's Dream*	• Hugh O'Neill, the Earl of Tyrone, rebels against British rule in Ireland. • Death of playwright Thomas Kyd.	• Sir Walter Raleigh explores the Orinoco.
1596	• *King John* • Shakespeare's son Hamnet dies, aged 11. • John Shakespeare granted coat of arms.	• "League of amity" between England and France. • Food riots in Kent and elsewhere, a result of one of England's worst known harvests. • Philip II of Spain sends a second armada against England. A storm scatters the fleet.	• Sir Francis Drake dies off the Panama coast.
1596–7	• *The Merchant of Venice* • *Henry IV, Part 1*		
1597	• Shakespeare buys New Place, one of the largest houses in Stratford-upon-Avon.	• The third Spanish armada is wrecked by storms.	
1597–8	• *The Merry Wives of Windsor* • *Henry IV, Part 2*		
1598	• *Much Ado About Nothing* • Court performance of Love's Labour's Lost.	• Death of William Cecil, Lord Burghley. • Irish rebels under Hugh O'Neill, the Earl of Tyrone, defeat the English at the Battle of Yellow Ford. • James VI of Scotland (James I of England) writes his treatise on the divine right of kings.	• Philip II of Spain dies. • Treaty of Nantes ends the French civil wars. The treaty granted religious toleration to Protestants.
1598–9	• *Henry V*		
1599	• The Globe Theatre built. • *Julius Caesar*	• Robert Devereux, Earl of Essex, is made Lord Lieutenant of Ireland. He arranges a truce with Hugh O'Neill. Returns to England without the Queen's permission.	
1599–1600	• *As You Like It*		
1600–1	• *Hamlet* • *Twelfth Night*		
1601	• Death of John Shakespeare. William Shakespeare inherits property in Henley Street.	• Essex Rebellion. *Richard II* performed at the Globe days before the rebellion. Essex is executed for treason.	
1602	• *Troilus and Cressida*		
1603	• The Lord Chamberlain's Men become the King's Men. • *Measure for Measure*	• Elizabeth I dies. James VI of Scotland ascends the English throne as James I. • Sir Walter Raleigh is arrested, tried and imprisoned for high treason. • Plague ravages London killing 33,000 people.	
1603–4	• *A Lover's Complaint* • *Sir Thomas More* • *Othello*		
1604–5	• *All's Well That Ends Well*		
1605	• *Timon of Athens*	• Gunpowder Plot foiled.	
1605–6	• *King Lear*		
1606	• *Macbeth* • *Antony and Cleopatra*	• London and Plymouth Companies receive charters to colonize Virginia.	• Rembrandt born.
1607	• Shakespeare's daughter Susanna marries John Hall, a Stratford physician. • Shakespeare's brother, Edmund, dies.		• Founding of the Jamestown Colony in Virginia by Captain John Smith.
1608	• *Coriolanus* • *Pericles* • Shakespeare's grand-daughter Elizabeth born to John and Susanna Hall. • Shakespeare's mother Mary dies. • The King's Men acquire an indoor theatre at Blackfriars.		
1609	• *The Winter's Tale*	• Plantation of Ulster begins, replacing Gaelic culture with English and Scottish culture.	• Moors expelled from Spain.
1610	• *Cymbeline*	• Prince Henry created Prince of Wales.	
1611	• *The Tempest*	• Publication of the King James version of the Bible.	
1612	• Death of Shakespeare's brother, Gilbert. • Death of Henry Wriothesley, Earl of Southampton.	• Execution of Lancashire witches.	
1613	• *Henry VIII (All is True)* • The Globe Theatre burns down during a performance of Henry VIII.		
1613–14	• *The Two Noble Kinsmen*		
1614	• The Globe Theatre rebuilt.	• Addled Parliament is summoned and dissolved, producing no legislation.	
1616	• Shakespeare's daughter Judith marries Thomas Quiney, a Stratford vintner. • Shakespeare dies, 23 April.	• Ben Jonson's plays published in Folio form.	

Item 1 – Shakespeare's Baptism Record

[1564] April 26 William son of John Shakespeare

Item 2 – Shakespeare's marriage bond

[English translation of the Latin]

Let all men know by these presents that we Fulke Sandells of Stratford in the County of Warwick, husbandman, and John Richardson there husbandman, are held and firmly bound by Richard Cosin gentleman and Robert Warmstry public notary to pay forty pounds of good and lawful money of England to the same Richard and Robert, their heirs, executors, or assigns: to make wich payment well and faithfully we bind ourselves and each of us severally for the whole and total amount, our heirs, executors, and administrators firmly by these presentes sealed with our seals. Given this day of November in the 25th year of the reign of our Lady Elizabeth, by the Grace of God Queen of England, France and Ireland, Defender of the Faith. &c

The condic[i]on of this obligac[i]on ys suche that it herafter there shall not appere any Lawfull Lett or impediment by reason of any p[re] contract consang[ui]nitie affinitie or by any other lawfull means whatsoeu[er] but that will[ia]m Shagspere one throne p[ar]tie, and Anne hathwey of Stratford in the Dioces of Worcester maiden may lawfully solennize m[at]ri[m]ony together and in the same afterward[es] remaine and continew like man and wife according vnto the lawes in that behalf prouided and moreou[er] if there be not at this p[re]sent time any action sute quarrel or demaund moved or depending befor any judge eccl[es]iasticall or temporall for and concerning any suche lawfull lett or impediment. And moreou[er] if the said will[ia]m Shagspere do not p[ro]cead to solennizac[i]on of marriadg with the said Anne hathwey without the consent of hir frind[es]. And also if the said will[ia]m do vpon his owne p[ro]per coste and expense defend & saue harmless the right Reverend father in god lord John bushop of Worcester and his officers for Licencing them the said will[ia]m and Anne to be married together with once asking of the bannes of m[at]ri[m]ony between them and for all other causes wch may ensue by reason or occasion therof that then the said obligac[i]on to be voyd and of none effect or els to stand and abide in full force and vertue

Item 3 – Baptism registration of Susanna Shakespeare

[1583] May 26 Susanna daughter to William Shakespeare

Item 4 – Baptism registration of Hamnet and Judith Shakespeare

[1585] Feb 2 Hamnet & Judeth sonne and daughter ~ to Willia Shakspere

Item 5 – Richard Quiney's letter to William Shakespeare asking for a loan

Loveinge Contreyman I am bolde of yow as of a ffrende, craveinge yowr helpe wth xxxli vppon mr Bushells & my securytee or mr wyttons wth me mr Rosswell is nott come to London as yeate & I have especiall cawse, yow shall ffrende me muche in helping me out of all the debett[es] I owe in London I thancke god and muche quiet my mynde wch wolde nott be indebeted I am nowe toward[es] the Cowrte in hope of answer for the dispatche of my Buysenes yow shall nether loase creddytt nor money by me the Lord wyllinge & nowe butt p[er]swade yowrselfe soe as I hope & yow shall nott need to feare butt wth all hartie thanckefullenes I wyll holde my tyme & content yowr ffrende & yf we Bargaine farther yow shalbe the paie mr yowrselfe, my tyme bidd[es] me hasten to an ende & soe I com[m]itt thys [to] yowr care & hope of yowr helpe I feare I shall nott be backe thys night ffrom the Cowrte. haste the Lord be wth yow & wth us all amen/ ffrom the Bell in Carter Lane the 25 octobr 1598/.

Yowrs in all kyndenes
Ric. Quyney

Item 8 – An account of Edmund Tylney, the Master of the Revels for the year 1 November 1604 to 31 October 1605 listing a number of Shakespeare's plays, all noted as being performed by His Majesty's Players, are listed below the date 1605 as follows (they comprise the first three entries, the fifth and the eighth):

On All Hallows' Day: The Moor of Venice (Othello)
The Sunday following: The Merry Wives of Windsor
On St Stephen's Night: Measure for Measure
On Innocent's Night: [The Comedy of] Errors
New Year's Day: Love's Labour's Lost

Item 10 – Letters Patent for King's Men from King James I

Right trusty and welbeloued Counsellor we greet you well and will and Com[m]annd you yt under o[ur] priuie Seale in yo[ur] Custody from the time being you Cause o[ur] le[tt]es to be made patent[es] in forme following. James by the grace of God king of England Scotland ffrance & Ireland defendor of the faith &c. To all Iustices Maio[rs] Sheriff[es] Constables Hedboroughes and other o[ur] officers and loving subiect[es] greeting. Know ye yt we of o[ur] speciall grace certaine knowledge & meere motion, haue licended and authorized & by these p[rese]nt[es] doe licence & authorize these o[ur] seruant[es] Lawrence ffletcher William Shakespeare Richard Burbage Augustine Phillipps John Hemming[es] Henry Condell William Sly Rob[er]t Armyn Richard Cowlye and the rest of their associat[es], freely to vse and exercise the Arte and facultie of playing Comedies Tradgedies Histories Enterludes Morall[es] Pastorall[es] Stage plaies & such other like as they haue already studied or hereafter shall vse or studie as well for the recreation of o[ur] loving subject[es] as for o[ur] solace and pleasure when we shall thinke good to see them during o[ur] pleasure And the said Comedies Tradgedies Histories Enterludes Morall[es] Pastorall[es] Stage plaies & such like To shew and exercise publiquely to their best Commoditie, when the infection of the plague shall decrease as well wit[h]in there now vsuall howse called the Globe wit[h]in o[ur] Countie of Surrey as also wit[h]in any towne Hall[es] or Mouthall[es] or other convenient places wit[h]in the liberties and freedome of any other Cittie Vniversitie Towne or Borough whatsoeu[er] wit[h]in o[ur] said Realms and dominions. Willing and Comaunding you and eu[er]ly of you as you tender o[ur] pleasure not only to p[er]mitt and suffer them heerin wi[t]hout any yo[ur] letts hinderances or molestac[i]ons during o[ur] said pleasure, but also to be ayding and assisting to them yf any wrong be to them offered And to allow them such former Courtesies as hathe bene giuen to men of their place and qualitie. And also what further fauo[er] you shall shew to these o[ur] seruant[es] for o[ur] sake we shall take kindely at yo[ur] hand[es] In witnes whereof And these o[ur] le[ttr]es shall be yo[ur] sufficient warrant and discharge in this behalf. Giuen vnder o[ur] Signet at o[ur] Manor of Greenewiche the seaventeenth day of May in the first yeere of o[ur] raigne of England ffraunce and Ireland, and of Scotland the six and thirtieth

ex[pedi]

p[er] Lake

[Reverse]

To our right trusty and welbeloued Counselor the Lord Cecill of Esingdon Keeper of our Priuy Seal for the time being.

Item 11 – An account of the Master of the Great Wardrobe recording the issue of red cloth to Shakespeare and his colleagues to make clothes to wear for the entry of King James I into London, 15 March 1604

[Then there are listed the several groups to whom allotments of scarlet-red cloth were made. On folio 78v are listed "fawkeners of Ordinary," "fawkeners," and then, on the bottom of folio 78v and, on the top of folio 79r, "Players"]:

Scarlet-Red cloth

William Shakespeare	iiij yard[es]	di[midium]
Augustine Phillips	iiij yard[es]	di[midium]
Lawrence ffletcher	iiij yard[es]	di[midium]
Players Iohn Hemming[es]		
	iiij yard[es]	di[midium]
Richard Burbage	iiij yard[es]	di[midium]

[the names continue at the top of folio 79r]

William Slye	iiij yard[es]	di[midium]
Robert Armyn	iiij yard[es]	di[midium]
Henry Cundell	iiij yard[es]	di[midium]
Richard Cowley	iiij yard[es]	di[midium]

Item 12 – Blackfriars Property Conveyance

This Indenture made the Tenthe day of March, in the yeare of our Lord god according to the Computac[i]on of the Church of England one thowsand six hundred and twelve, and in the yeares of the reigne of our Sovereigne Lord Iames by the grace of god king of England, Scotland ffraunce, and Ireland defender of the faithe &c that is to saie of England, ffraunce, and Ireland the tenth, and of Scotland the six and fortith; Betweene Henry Walker Citizein and Minstrell of London of th'one partie, And William Shakespeare of Stratford vpon Avon in the countie of Warwick gentleman, William Iohnson Citizein and Vintener of London, Iohn Jackson, and Iohn Hem[m]yng of London gentleman of th'other partie. Witnesseth that the said Henry Walker (for and in considerac[i]on of the som[m]e of one hundred and fortie pound[es] of lawfull money of England to him in the hande before th'ensealing hereof by the said William Shakespeare well and trulie paid, whereof, and wherewith hee the said Henry Walker doth acknowledge himselfe fullie satisfied and contented, and thereof, and of every part and parcel thereof doth doth cleerlie acquite and discharge the said William Shakespeare his heirs, executo[ur]s, administrato[ur]s, and assignes, and every of them by theis p[rese]ntes) Hath bargained & soulde and by theis p[rese]ntes doth fullie cleerlie, and absolutlie bargayne and sell vnto the said William Shakespeare, William Iohnson, Iohn Jackson, and Iohn Hem[m]yng their heirs, and assignes forever, All that dwelling house or Tenement wth th'appurten[au]nc[es] situate and being within the Precinct, Circuit and Compasse of the late black ffryers London,

Item 13 – Shakespeare's Will

Vicesimo Quinto die ~~Ianuarij~~ m[ar]tij Anno Regni D[omi]ni nri[?] Iacobi nunc R[eginis] Anglie &c decimo quarto & Scotie xlixo Annoq[ue] d[omi]ni 1616

T~~w~~mj Shackspeare/

R r In the name of god Amen I Willi[a]m Shackspeare of Stratford vpon Avon in the countie of warr[wick] gent[leman] in p[er]fect health & memorie god be praysed Doe make & Ordayne this my last will & testam[en]t in mann[er] & forme followeing That ys to saye ffirst I Comend My Soule into the hand[es] of god my Creator hoping & assuredlie believing through thronlie Meritt[es] of Iesus Christe my Saviour to be made p[ar]taker of lyfe everlastinge And my bodye to the Earth whereof yt ys made It[e]m I Gyve & bequeath vnto my ~~sonne in L~~ daughter Judyth One Hundred & ffyftie pound[es] of lawful English money to be paied vnto her in mann[er] & forme followeing That ys to saye One Hundred Pound[es] in discharge of her marriage pore[i]on w[i]thin one yeare after my deceas w[i]th considerac[i]on after the Rate of twoe shilling[es] in the pound for soe long tyme as the same shallbe vnpaied vnto her after my deceas & the ffyftie pound[es] Residewe thereof vpon her Surrendring of or giving of such sufficient securitie as the overseers of this my Will shall like of to Surrender or gr[a]unte All her estate & Right that shall discend or come vnto her after my deceas or ~~that she~~ nowe hath of in or to one Copiehold ten[emen]te w[i]th thapp[ur]ten[au]nc[es] lyeing & being in Stratford vpon Avon ~ aforesaid in the saied countie of warr[wick] being p[ar]cell or holden of the mann[or] of Rowington vnto my

Daughter Susanna Hall & her heirs for ever It[e]m I Gyve & bequeath vnto my saied Daughter Judith One ~ Hundred & ffyftie Pound[es] more if she or Anie issue of her bodie be Lyvinge att thend of three Yeares next ensueing the daie of the Date of this my will during w[hi]ch tyme my execut[rs] to paie her considerac[i]on from my deceas according to the Rate aforesaied And if she dye w[i]thin the saied terme w[i]thout issue of her bodye then my will ys & I doe gyve & bequeath One Hundred Pound[es] thereof to my Neece Elizabeth Hall & the ffiftie Pound[es] to be sett fourth by my execuo[rs] During the life of my Sister Johane Harte & vse & p[ro]ffitt thereof Cominge shalbe payed to my saied Sister Jone and after her deceas the saied 1li shall Remaine Amongst the children of my saied Sister Jone to be Devided Amongst them But if my saied Daughter Judith be lyving att thend of the saied three Years or anie yssue of her bodye then my will ys & soe I Devise and bequeath the saied Hundred and ffyftie pound[es] to be sett out ~~by my executo[rs] & overseers~~ for the best benefit of her & her issue & the stock not paied vnto her soe long as she shalbe marryed & Covert Baron ~~by my executo[rs] & overseers~~ but my will ys that she shall have the considerac[i]on yearelie paied vnto her during her life & after her deceas the saied stock and considerac[i]on to bee paied to her children id she have Anie & if not to her execuo[rs] or assignes she lyving the saied terme after my deceas Provided that id such husbond as she shall att thend of saied three Years be marryed vnto or att anie [tyme] after doe sufficientlie Assure vnto her & thissue of her bodie land[es] Awnswereable to the porc[i]on by this my will given vnto her & to be adiudged soe by my executo[rs] ~ & overseers then my will ys that the saied Cli shalbe paied to such husbond as shall make such assurance to his owne vse It[e]m I gyve & bequeath vnto my saied sister Jone xxli & all my wearing apparell to be paied & deliu[er]ed w[i]thin one yeare after my deceas And I William Shakspere doe will & devise vnto her the house w[i]th thapp[ur]ten[au]nc[es] in Stratford wherein she dwelleth for her naturall life vnder the yearelie Rent of xijd It[e]m I Gyve & bequeath

[Sheet 2]

vnto her three sonns Welli[a]m Harte [Thomas] hart & Michael Harte ffyve pound[es] A peece to be payed w[i]thin one Yeare after my deceas ~~to be sett out for her w[i]thin one Yeare after my Deceas by my executo[rs] W[i]th thadvise & direcc[i]ons of my overseers for her best p[ro]ffitt vntill her ~ Marriage & then the same w[i]th the increase thereof to be paied vnto her~~ It[e]m I gyve & bequeath vnto ~~her~~ All my Plate ~~the saied~~ Elizabeth Hall (except my brod silver and gilt bole) that I now have att the Date of this my will It[e]m I gyve & bequeath vnto the Poore of Stratford aforesaid tenn pound[es] to m[aste]r Thomas Combe my Sword to Thomas Russell Esquier ffyve pound[es] & to ffrauncis Collins of the Borough of warr[wick] in the countie of warr[wick] gent[leman] thirteene pound[es] Sixe shilling[es] & Eight pence to be paied w[i]thin one Yeare after my Deceas It[e]m I gyve & bequeath to m[aste]r ~~Richard Tyler~~ Hamlett Sadler theld[er] xxvj^s viij^d to buy him A Ringe to willi[a]m Raynold[es] gent[leman] xxvj^s viij^d to buy him A Ringe to my godson Will[ia]m Walker xx^s in gold to Anthonye Nashe gent[leman] xxvj^s viij^d & to M[aste]r John Nashe xxvj^s ~~in gold~~ & to my ffellowes Iohn Hemyng[es] Richard Burbage & Henry Cundell xxvj^s viij^d A peece to buy them Ring[es] viijd It[e]m I gyve ~~Will~~ bequeath & Devise vnto my Daughter Susanna Hall for better enabling of her to p[er]forme this my will and toward[es] the p[er]formans thereof All that Capitall Messuage or ten[emen]te w[i]th in Stratford aforesaid thapp[ur]ten[au]nc[es] Called the newe place wherein I nowe Dwell & twoe messuag[es] or ten[emen]tes w[i]th

thapp[ur]ten[au]nc[es] scituat lyeing & being in Henley streete w[i]th^in the borough of Stratford aforesaied And all my barnes stables Orchard[es] gardens land[es]ten[emem]t[es] & hereditam[en]t[es] whatsoev[er] scituat lyeing & being or to be had Receyved p[er]ceyved or taken w[i]th^in the townes Hamlett[es] villag[es] ffield[es] & ground[es] of Stratford vpon Avon Oldstratford Bushopton & welcombe or in anie of themin the saied countie of warr[wick] And alsoe All that Messuage or ten[emen]te w[i]th thapp[ur]ten[au]nc[es] wherein one John Robinson Dwelleth scituat lyeing & being in the blackfriers in London ncre the Wardrobe and all oth[er] my land[es]

ten[emen]t[es] & hereditam[en]t[es] whatsoeu[er] To Have & to hold All & sing[u]ler the saied p[re]miss[es] w[i]th their App[ur]ten[au]nc[es] vnto the saied Susanna Hall for & During the terme of her naturall lief & after her ~ Deceas to the first sonne of her bodie lawfullie yssueing & for Defalt of such issue to the second Sonne of her bodie lawfullie yssueinge & so to the heires Males of the bodie of the saied Second Sonne lawfullie yssueinge & for defalt of such heirs to the third Sonne of the bodie of the saied Susanna ~ Lawfullie ysseuing & of the heires Males of the bodie of the saied third sonne lawfullie yssueing And for Defalt of such issue the same soe to be & Remaine to the ffourth ~~sonne~~ ffyfth sixte & Seaventh ~ sonnes of her bodie lawfullie issueing one after Anoth[er] &to the heires

Willi[a]m Shakspere

[Sheet 3]

Males of the bodies of the bodies of the saied fourth fifth Sixte & Seaventh sonnes lawfullie yssueing, in such manner as yt ys before Lymitted to be & Remaine to the first second and third Sonns of her bodie & to their heires Males; And for defalt of such issue the said premisses to be & Remaine to my sayed Neece Hall & the heires males of her bodie Lawfullie yssueinge, and for defalt of such issue to my daughter Judith and the heires Males of her bodie lawfullie yssueinge, and for defalt of such issue to the Right heires of me the saied William Shackspare for ever. I gyve vnto my wife my second best bed with the furniture, I gyve & bequeath to my saied daughter Judith my broad silver gilt bole. All the Rest of my goodes chattels leases plate jewels & household stuffe whatsoever, after my dettes and Legasies paied and my funerall expences discharged, I give devise and bequeath to my Sonne in Lawe, John Hall gent & my daughter Susanna his wife whom I ordaine & make executours of this my Last will and testament. And I doe intreat & Appoint the saied Thomas Russell Esquier & ffrauncis Collins gent to be overseers hereof. And doe Revoke All former wills & publishe this to be my last will and testament. In witnesse whereof I have hereunto put my [seale] hand, the daie & Yeare first above Written. witnes to the publyshing by me William Shakespeare hereof.
Fra: Collyns
Julyus Shawe
John Robinson
Hamnet Sadler
Robert Whattcott

Item 14 – Registration of Shakespeare's burial:

[1616] April 25 will Shakspere gent

FURTHER READING

SHAKESPEARE'S LIFE
• *1599: A Year in the Life of William Shakespeare* by James Shapiro, Faber and Faber, London, 2005
• *In Search of Shakespeare* by Michael Wood, BBC Books, London, 2003
• *Shakespeare: A Dramatic Life* by Stanley Wells, Sinclair-Stevenson, London, 1994
• *Shakespeare: A Life* by Park Honan, Oxford University Press, Oxford, 1998
• *Ungentle Shakespeare: Scenes from his Life* by Katherine Duncan-Jones, Arden Shakespeare, London, 2001

SHAKESPEARE'S THEATRE
• *Looking at Shakespeare: A Visual History of Twentieth-Century Performance* by Dennis Kennedy, Cambridge University Press, Cambridge, 2001
• *The Oxford Illustrated History of Shakespeare on Stage* by Jonathan Bate and Russell Jackson, Oxford University Press, Oxford, 2001
• *Playgoing in Shakespeare's London* by Andrew Gurr, Cambridge University Press, Cambridge, 2004
• *Shakespeare and the Drama of his Time* by Martin Wiggins, Oxford University Press, Oxford, 2000

SHAKESPEARE'S TEXTS
• Arden, Cambridge University Press, Oxford University Press and Penguin publish the most authoritative editions of single plays.
• Editions of the Collected Works are published by Arden, Norton, Oxford University Press and Riverside.

SHAKESPEARE'S LEGACY
• *After Shakespeare: Writing Inspired by the World's Greatest Author* by John Gross, Oxford University Press, Oxford, 2002
• *Shakespearean Afterlives: Ten Characters with a Life of their Own* by John O'Connor, Icon, Cambridge, 2003
• *Reinventing Shakespeare: A Cultural History from the Restoration to the Present* by Gary Taylor, Vintage, London, 1991

CHILDREN'S BOOKS ON SHAKESPEARE
• *Mr William Shakespeare's Plays* by William Shakespeare, Walker Books, London, 2000
• *Shakespeare for Kids: His Life and Times* by Collen Aagesen, Margie Blumberg, Chicago Review Press, Chicago, 1999
• *The Timetraveller's Guide to Shakespeare's London* by Joshua Doder, Watling St Ltd, London, 2004
• *Top Ten Shakespeare Stories* by Terry Deary, Scholastic, London, 1998

WEBSITES
The websites of the Shakespeare Birthplace Trust and the Royal Shakespeare Company offer reliable information and are useful sources for illustrations, performances, and educational materials:
www.shakespeare.org.uk
www.rsc.org.uk

INDEX

Numbers in Italics indicate illustrations

PUBLISHERS' ACKNOWLEDGEMENTS

Carlton Books would like to thank the following for their help in the production of this book: Andrew Edwards at the Royal Shakespeare Company; Dr Robert Bearman, Karin Brown, Adam Graham, Helen Hargest, Sylvia Morris and Jo Wong and colleagues at the Shakespeare Birthplace Trust and Records Office.

Extra special thanks to David Howells, Curator, and Helen Robson of the Royal Shakespeare Company for their patience and hard work behind the scenes.

PICTURE CREDITS
The publishers would like to thank the following sources for their kind permission to reproduce the pictures in this book.

Abbreviations
BAL = Bridgeman Art Library
MEPL = Mary Evans Picture Library
RGA = Ronald Grant Archive
RSC = The Royal Shakespeare Company
SBT = The Shakespeare Birthplace Trust

1: RSC,: 2/3: BAL/®Yale Center for British Art, Paul Mellon Fund, USA; 4: (cr) BAL/Nicholas Hilliard/Berkeley Castle, Gloucestershire, (cl) BAL/Nicholas Hilliard/Walker Art Gallery, National Museums, Liverpool, (tr)Topfoto, (b) Topfot/Fotomas, (tl & cl) Topfoto/Public Record Office/HIP;4/5: (b) Topfoto/RHR, 5: (tl) MEPL, (tr) Topfoto/RHR, (background) Corbis,6: (tl & tr) MEPL, (r) MEPL, (b) National Portrait Gallery, London;7: (tr) MEPL, (tl) Topfoto/ Fotomas, (b) Topfot/Fotomas, (background) Topfoto/Fotomas; 8: (tr) Vanessa Daubney, with kind permission of Stratford-upon-Avon Town Trust, (l) Topfoto/Spectrum Colour Library, (b) Topfoto/ Woodmansterne, (background) MEPL; 9: (t) MEPL/Bruce Castle Museum, (b) National Trust Photo Library, (r) Topfoto//PAL, (cl) Topfoto/Woodmansterne;10: (b) Rex Features/Nicholas Bailey, (tl) Vanessa Daubney, with kind permission of Stratford-upon-Avon Town Trust, (tr) Vanessa Daubney, with kind permission of the Dean and Chapter of Southwark; 11: (tr) MEPL, (bl) National Trust Photo Library, (backgroud) National Trust Photo Library, (tl) Topfoto; 12/13:(b) Topfoto/Corporation of London/HIP; 12: (tr) MEPL,(tl) BAL/studio of Daniel Mytens/Private Collection, Philip Mould, Historical Portraits Ltd, London, (br) BAL/Joris Hoefnagel/Hatfield House, Hertfordshire, (bl) Topham Picturepoint;13: (tc & tl) MEPL, (tr) BAL/John de Critz the Elder/Boughton House, Northamptonshire, (bl) BAL/WIlliam Larkin/Audley End, Essex; 14/15: (background) RSC/Giles Keyte, (b) RSC/Reg Wilson; 14: (br) MEPL, (bl) RSC/ Reg Wilson;15: (tl)Private Collection, (tr) SBT, (b) Topfoto;16: (tl) Topfoto, (r) Topfoto/Corporation of London/HIP, (br) Topfoto, (bl) BAL/Eugene Delacroix/Musée des Beaux-Arts, Reims, France; 17: (tl) Corbis Images/David Cummings/Eye Ubiquitous, (tr) Topfot, (b) BAL/Victoria & Albert Museum, London, (br) RSC/Reg Wilson; 18: (r) RSC, (br) Topfoto, (bl) RSC, (br) Topfoto, (background)British Library; 19: (t) Topfoto/Fotomas, (bl) RSC/Manuel Harlan, (c) BAL/ Private Collection, Giraudon, France, (br) Topfoto; 20: (tl) RSC/W & D Downey, (r) RSC/William H. Sullivan, (b) SBT/Malcolm Davies Collection; 21: (tl) Courtesy of Folger Shakespeare Library, Washington, (tr) Topfoto/ArenaPAL, (bl) RSC/Angus McBean, (br) RSC/Reg

Wilson; 22: (br) MEPL, (tl) RSC, (bl) BAL/Biblioteca Marciana, Venice, Italy/Giraudon, France, (tr) Topfoto; 23: (tr) Private Collection, (tl, tcl & tcr) RSC, (bl) SBT/Malcolm Davies Collection, (br) SBT/ Joe Cocks Studio Collection; 24: (tl) RSC/Angus McBean, (tc & b) RSC, (tr)Topfoto; 25: (tr) SBT/Malcolm Davies Collection, (tl) SBT/Reg Wilson, (cl) RSC, (bl) RSC/Alix Stone, (bcr & br) SBT/ Malcolm Davies Collection, (bcl) SBT/The Thos. F. and Mig Holte Photographic Collection; 26: (tl) BAL/William Hogarth/Walker Art Gallery, National Museum, Liverpool, (tr) BAL/Centre Historique des Archives Nationales, Paris, France/Archives Charmet (bl) Corbis Images/Godfrey Thurston Hopkins/Hulton-Deutsch Collection, (bc) RSC, (br & background) Topfoto/Fotomas; 27: (tl) RSC/Reg Wilson, (tr & background) BAL/engraved by Edward Fisher/after Jean Baptiste Vanloo/Private Collection, (bl) RSC/J. Dockar-Drysdale, (br) RSC/ John Haynes, (bc) RSC/Reg Wilson; 28: (tl) BAL/Victoria and Albert Museum, London, (tr) Corbis Images/Hulton-Deutsch/Gordon Anthony, (br) RSC, (bl) Topfoto/Michael Ward; 29: (tl) RSC, (tr) SBT/ Joe Cocks Studio Collection, (bl) RSC, (br) SBT/Malcolm Davies Collection; 30: (tl) BAL/James Northcote/Manchester Art Gallery, (tr) Topfoto, (c) RSC, (b) Shakespeare Theatre Company, Washington, USA/Carol Rosegg,; 31: (tl) RSC/Reg Wilson, (tr) BAL/Benjamin Wilson/®Yale Center for British Art, Paul Mellon Collection, USA, Paul Mellon Fund, (bl) RSC/Reg Wilson, (br) RSC/Manuel Harlan, (cl) University of Birmingham/The University of Birmingham Collections; 32: (tl) Topfoto, (tr) MEPL, (bl) RSC/Angus McBean, (br) RSC/John Bury, (c) SBT/Joe Cocks Studio Collection; 33: (tl) RSC/ Angus McBean, (tr & background) Rex Features/Everett Collection, (cl) RSC, (bl) RSC/Donald Cooper, (br) RSC/Reg Wilson; 34: (t) Alastair Muir, (l) Thelma Holt Limited, (bl) RSC/Manuel Harlan (br) MEPL; 35: (tl) SBT/Reg Wilson, (tr) AKG London, (bl) Corbis Images/Condé Nast Archive/Cecil Beaton, (c) SBT/Joe Cocks Studio Collection, (br) Topfoto; 36/37: (b) RSC/Reg Wilson;36: (t) RSC/ Angus McBean, (b) RSC/Reg Wilson; 37: (tl) RSC/Joe Cocks, (tr) BAL/Private Collection, (bc) AKG London/Sotheby's, (br) MEPL, (background) Topfoto/Public Records Office; 38: (tl) BAL/Hilliard/ Victoria and Albert Museum, London, (tr) AKG London, (b) RSC/ Reg Wilson, (background) RSC; 39: (tl) BAL/Titian/Musée des Beaux-Arts, Bordeaux,France/Giraudon, (tr) AKG London/Erich Lessing, (bl) RSC, (bc) BAL/Lambeth Palace, London, (br) BAL/John Critz/Private Collection; 40/41: MEPL; 40: (tl) Topfoto/Clive Barda/ ArenaPAL, (tr) Topfot/Hogarth/Specturm Colour Library, (b) AKG London/Jan Claesz Visscher/British Library; 41: (tl) RSC, (tr) AKG London, (bl) Chatsworth/The Devonshire Collection, Chatsworth. Reproduced by permission of the Chatsworth Settlement Trustees; 42: (t) Topfoto, (r) Topfoto/The British Library/HIP/George Vertue, (bl) Rex Features/Jonathan Leigh; 43: (tl) Rex Features/Richard Gardner, (tr) Topfoto/Woodmansterne, (b) Corbis Images/Dean Conger, (bakcgournd) Topfoto; 44: (tl) MEPL, (tr) Corbis Images/ Michael Nicholson, (b)BAL/The Holburne Museum of Art, Bath; 45: (tl) MEPL (tc) Corbis Images/Historical Pictures Archive, (tr) Topfoto, (bl) Topfoto (br) BAL/Pieter Van Bleeck/®Yale Center for British Art, Paul Mellon Collection, USA; 46: (tl) Corbis Images/Bettmann, (tr) Topfoto/Fotomas, (b) Topfoto/Ann Ronan Picture Library, (background)Corbis Images/Historical Picture Archive;47: (tcl & background)Corbis Images/Stapleton Collection,(cr) Corbis Images/

Bettmann, (c, cl & cr) MEPL, (b) RSC; 48: (tl) SBT, (tc) Corbis Images, (tr) MEPL, (bl & background) Corbis Images/Historical Picture Archive, (br) RSC; 49: (tl) Topfoto, (tr) Corbis Images/Bettmann, (cl) Corbis/Hulton-Deutsch Collection, (b) Topfoto; 50: (tl) Mander and Mitchenson, (tr) Corbis Images/John Springer Collection, (c) Birmingham City Council/reproduced by permission of Birmingham Library and Information services and the Sir Barry Jackson Trust, (bl) Corbis Images/Hulton-Deutsch Collection, (bc) Rex Features/ Guy Drayton, (br) RSC/Reg Wilson; 51: (tl) RSC/Reg Wilson, (tc) Corbis Images/Pierre Vauthey/Corbis Sygma, (tr) Craig Holmes/Loop Images/Corbis, (b) RSC/Reg Wilson; 52/53: Comedie Francaise/ Musée de la Comedie-Francaise; 52: (tl) SBT, (tr) Corbis Images/ Archivio Iconografico, S.A., (cl) SBT, (c) RSC, (br) Corbis Images/ Kaveh Kazemi, (bl) Stratford Festival Archives, Ontario;53: (t) Folger Shakespeare Library, Washington, (br) Corbis Images/Adrian Dennis/ EPA, (bl) Ruphin Coudyzer; 54: (tl) RGA, (tr) RGA/Alpine Films, (bl) AKG London/United Artists/Album, (br) Corbis Images/John Springer Collection;55: (tl) RGA, (tc) Topfoto, (tr) AKG, (l)Rex Features/SNAP, (b) RGA/Two Cities; 56: (tl) RGA/Filmways, (tr) RGA/Castle Rock Entertainment, (bl) RGA/Lenfilm, (bc) RGA/ Toho, (br) Corbis Images/Sunset Boulevard; 57: (t) RGA/Bazmark, (cl) Corbis Images/Sygma,, (cr) Corbis Images/Christopher Felver, (bl) Corbis Images/Bureau L.A. Collection, (br) RGA/Titus Productions; 58: (tl)The Advertising Archive Ltd, (tr) Corbis Images/Robbie Jack, (bl) Picture Desk/The Art Archive, (br) AKG London/Erich Lessing; 59: (tl) Corbis Images/Roger Wood, (tc) Corbis Images/Hulton-Deutsch Collection, (tr) Topfoto, (l) Corbis Images/Fabian Cevallos; 60/61: RSC; 62/63: RSC; 64: Warwickshire County Records Office.

Every effort has been made to acknowledge correctly and contact the source and/or copyright holder of each picture and Carlton Books Limited apologizes for any unintentional errors or omissions which will be corrected in future editions of this book.

MEMORABILIA CREDITS
All facsimile memorabilia has been reproduced by kind permission of the following:

Bishop of Worcester: Item 2; Kandis Cook: Item 20; The National Archives: Items 8, 10, 11, 12 and 13; Royal Shakespeare Company: Items 6 (pages 1, 2, 3 and 6), 7, 9 and 15; Shakespeare Birthplace Trust and Records Office: Items 1, 3, 4, 5, 6 (cover, pages 4 and 5), 14, 16, 17, 18 and 19.